for Nina

CARNEGIE PUBLIC LIBRARY
ROBINSON, ILLINOIS

Saturday's Child

Monday's child is fair of face,
Tuesday's child is full of grace,
Wednesday's child is full of woe,
Thursday's child has far to go,
Friday's child is loving and giving,
Saturday's child works hard for a living,
But a child that's born on the Sabbath day
Is fair and wise and good and gay.

OLD NURSERY RHYME

Saturday's Child

36 WOMEN TALK ABOUT THEIR JOBS

INTERVIEWS AND PHOTOGRAPHS BY SUZANNE SEED

J. PHILIP O'HARA, INC.
CHICAGO

CARNEGIE PUBLIC LIBRARY
ROBINSON, ILLINOIS

Library of Congress Cataloging in Publication Data

Seed, Suzanne. Saturday's child.

   SUMMARY: Women from such field as the arts, communication, science, business, and government discuss their jobs, job requirements, and job selection.
1. Woman—Employment—Juvenile literature.
2. Occupations—Juvenile literature. [1. Woman—Employment. 2. Occupations]
I. Title.
HD6058.S46   331.4   72-12599
ISBN 0-87955-803-2
ISBN 0-87955-203-4 (pbk)

© 1973 by Suzanne Seed.

All rights reserved. Nothing herein may be reproduced in any form without written permission from the publisher. Manufactured in the United States of America.

J. Philip O'Hara, Inc., 20 East Huron, Chicago, 60611. Published simultaneously in Canada by Van Nostrand Reinhold Ltd., Scarborough, Ontario.

First Printing B

CONTENTS

ARTS & COMMUNICATIONS
Architect	12
Conductor, Composer, Pianist	16
Sportswriter	21
Dress Designer	24
Painter	27
Theater Director	31
Radio-TV Reporter	36
Film Maker	41
Actress	45
Illustrator	48

SCIENCE & MEDICINE
Veterinarian	52
Geologist	57
Physician	62
Oceanographer	65
Pharmacist	70
Physician's Associate	74
Developmental Biologist	79
Biophysicist	83

TRADES, SERVICES & BUSINESSES
Letter Carrier	88
Pilot	91
Carpenter	94
Policewoman	98
Florist	101
Cab Driver	104
Realtor	108
Telephone Repairwoman	111

COMMERCE & GOVERNMENT
Congresswoman	116
Commodities Broker	121
Accountant	125
City Planner	128
Brigadier General	131
Lawyer	135
Marketing Executive	140
Industrial Psychologist	143
Systems Analyst	146
Bank Vice-President	151

For Further Information	154
Author/Photographer	157
Index	159

Author's Note

He who has a trade, has a share everywhere.
He who has an art, has everywhere a part.

Thomas Fuller

In the days when these sayings originated, there were not many different trades or arts. Today, there are thousands of interesting occupations open to both men and women. We can now add that *she* who has a trade has a share everywhere, and *she* who has an art, has everywhere a part.

You already know what women do in the fields of nursing and teaching, but if you have never met a woman carpenter, veterinarian, pilot, geologist, or sportswriter, you will meet them here. The things they tell about their work are things girls have asked to know.

Most of the particular fields included in this book were chosen because studies show that there may be more growth in these fields than in others. There will be a growing need for people in trades, sciences, medicine and services. Hopefully there will be a greater need for talented people in the arts. But some of the fields most popular with girls in the past are expected to be overcrowded in the future. There will be fewer openings for dieticians, stewardesses, teachers and librarians.

Although all of the many jobs available are not included in this book, visiting with the women here can give you clues about how one gets a start in most kinds of work. Even if some of the fields in this book do not interest you, there is general information that should be of help in anyone's life and work.

By reading how the women discovered their chosen fields, you may learn how to read the signs of a budding talent in yourself, how to grasp an opportunity when it arises, or how to seek training in a field that interests you. Most important, you may learn how to determine your strongest talents. It's likely that you will have a job for some part of your life. Everyone is happiest at work that uses his or her special abilities. A girl who thinks that she has no special abilities hasn't had a chance to look hard enough, for everyone does some one particular thing better than others.

If you are one of those who finds and uses her abilities, work can help you discover yourself and give you a share everywhere.

ARTS & COMMUNICATIONS

Gertrude Lempp Kerbis ARCHITECT

When I was eighteen I took off for college without the slightest notion of what I wanted to be. I did know that I loved both science and art, but didn't think I could combine them in one field; they didn't seem to go together. So I studied liberal arts, took both science and art courses, and wondered what on earth I would be when I graduated.

One day a friend happened to mention a school about fifty miles away from ours—a private school called Taliesin East run by the architect Frank Lloyd Wright. My friend spoke of how unusual the school was and how beautiful the buildings were. They had all been designed by Wright.

On a whim I decided to see the school. I hitchhiked, which was not as dangerous then as it is now, and got a ride in a truck. The driver pointed out the school when we came near enough to see it. Although it was still miles away, I was so excited and nervous about hitchhiking that I jumped out right there, several miles from Taliesin, though it looked close. After an hour's walk I finally reached it but could find no way in, so I climbed a wall. The place seemed to be completely deserted and I roamed the grounds, awed by the beautiful architecture surrounding me. It fit the grounds so exquisitely and suggested a very special way of life. Caught up in my thoughts, I suddenly heard heavy, clumsy footsteps behind me. It flashed through my mind that I was a trespasser! Were these watchdogs or guards? I turned to discover I was being followed by several large peacocks that seemed to be living on the grounds. Relieved, I realized that I was very tired. Since it was evening, and I was far from anywhere, I climbed into one of the buildings through a window. I fell asleep, hoping to find someone in the morning. When I woke, I noticed that the interior of the building was as beautifully designed as the exterior, and different from any I had seen before. It occurred to me that it had taken both science and art to build these structures, that as an architect one would use both.

A little later, I finally found the caretaker's cottage and he informed me that Mr. Wright and the students had gone to another

part of the school hundreds of miles away, called Taliesin West. I hurried back to my own school, anxious to change my major to architecture immediately. My school didn't teach it, so I transferred to Harvard to study design, then to Illinois Institute of Technology to study architecture and planning. I never met Frank Lloyd Wright until I was already an architect.

There are few women in this field, and I've never been sure just why. Women have a feeling for beautiful buildings and a sense of what kinds of space are right for various activities. These are major considerations in architecture. I've met many girls who like both science and art, but who hadn't imagined themselves as architects. I encourage them to consider the field.

According to some scientists, architecture was invented by women. They believe that in prehistoric times, while a caveman was out hunting animals, the cavewoman would build structures to protect her young—in the way animals build nests. This would have been necessary because there were not caves in all the places where prehistoric people lived. As the cavewomen perfected her protective structures, they would have become more and more like huts, or houses.

The sooner there are more women in this field, the sooner those who hire architects will get used to them. This was a problem for me at first, for most of the people I worked with had never met a woman architect. For this reason, I took a job in a large architectural firm when I first graduated, to have the security of a large firm behind me. Just a few years ago, I took a giant step and opened my own firm.

For me, the most interesting part of architecture is the chance to invent new ways of solving problems, using science to do what seems impossible. For the dining building of the U. S. Air Force Academy, I had the roof built on the ground and raised into place with hydraulic lifts.

To me, architecture is a way of creating space. The building materials used are there primarily to create an interior space. The exterior must be beautiful too, but must be determined by the space it is creating. When you see a building, you *see* walls, floors, and ceilings, but what you *feel* is the shape of the space you are in—how big that space is, how airy, how simple or mysterious.

Although the challenge of creating new solutions to building problems is exciting, for me the greatest satisfaction comes when the building is finished and I can watch people walking through a structure that once existed only in my mind.

Margaret Harris CONDUCTOR, COMPOSER, PIANIST

My mother always devoted a certain time of day to me alone when I was a child. From the time I was a baby, at that certain time she would play the piano and sing for me, putting me on the piano bench next to her when I was old enough to sit up. One day when she was too busy to do it, I crawled up on the bench and began to pick out "Mary Had A Little Lamb." Mother came running in from the kitchen and saw me at the piano, but thought it must have been some fluke that allowed me to play, for I was only two and a half years old. So she asked me to play it again for her. I played it again and again, first for her, then for my godmother whom she called over.

Having foresight, my mother realized that I would need to read music and since I really seemed to like it, I should have lessons. So I learned to read music and by the time I was three had learned enough for a concert, which my teacher arranged. Naturally it caused a big to-do because I was so young. My mother decided she would have to take care that I was not spoiled or exploited. She explained to me that this situation was most unusual, but that did not make me a special-special child. Mother is a very religious person, and I was taught that the talent I had was loaned to me while I'm on earth, that it was passing through me to others. That while I'm here I should use it to the best of my ability and it would not die with me, but be passed on like a torch in the Olympics. It may sound strange, but that's what I believe. And when my playing and compositions make people happy, I feel in some way like a missionary, which is what my mother had wanted me to be.

When I was older I went to the Juilliard School of Music. I kept on with the piano, but felt the need to know music from other perspectives. So I studied composing to find out what goes into a piece and conducting so I'd know what was going on with each part of an orchestra when I performed with one. Both of these areas have since become as much a part of my life as performing, and I can't tell which I enjoy most. Perhaps I should describe each separately.

In conducting, the greatest satisfaction comes from working with the musicians in the orchestra, seeing smiles on their faces,

knowing they want to please me. And I know they don't want to please me just to get me out of their hair, for I'm not an authoritarian figure to them. I'm someone with whom they're making music. It's a nice, warm kind of feeling to look out on the orchestra and see all eyes on you, waiting to make music with you and looking to you to help them do it well.

The achievement I'm most proud of has come to me through conducting, and that was being able to conduct a major American symphony orchestra. Frankly, I think that fifteen years ago it would never have happened. We've had black conductors, but they've all been men. To be the first black woman conductor is an experience I value. Since my U. S. debut with the Chicago Symphony Orchestra, I've been a guest conductor with the Los Angeles Philharmonic and soon will conduct the St. Louis, Minneapolis, and San Diego symphonies as guest conductor. I have also served as musical director and conductor for the musical, *Hair,* in New York City.

My big break into conducting had come before any of this, and completely out of the blue! I had been asked at the last minute to replace a pianist in a European tour of a show called *Black New World.* I was thrilled to be going to Europe and very happy with the job. On the plane next day, the producer walked over to me looking very distressed. I asked him what was wrong, and he said it was *another* last-minute cancellation—this time the conductor. "You saw the rehearsal yesterday, didn't you?" he said. I admitted I had. "You studied choral and orchestral conducting in school, didn't you?" I told him that was right. "Good," he said, "you're our conductor—here's the score for you to study. We open almost as soon as we arrive." So I made my European debut conducting orchestra, chorus, and cuing dancers—with no rehearsal. It was just like those old movies where a director says, "The star broke her leg, get the understudy to replace her. The show must go on!"

Most people associate batons with conducting, but I'm impatient with them, and whenever possible, I avoid using them. Holding a baton uses nearly the whole hand and keeps it stiff. The hand is so much more flexible and expressive without it, for obviously, you can do more with ten fingers than five.

In composing, the greatest enjoyment for me comes with hearing a piece of mine performed for the first time. Some parts sound different than I think they will and some are better than I expect. Whole new ideas emerge and I can't wait to get back to the piece and rework it. Most of all, it's exciting to hear a full orchestra of perhaps one hundred and six instruments playing a work that you've been alone with up till then. It gives me goosebumps.

There's great challenge in composition: you must be independent, think on your own terms and be able to defend what you write. This has given some people the impression that it's a masculine field which is just not true.

In composing music, I have many elements to draw on. There's my background in performing and conducting, and also the ethnic thing. I'm close to black musical forms while my training is in the classical tradition. I like melodic music that reaches the heart. Recently I completed a concerto scored for piano with full symphony orchestra plus electric bass and trap drum. It's a rhythm concerto, not a rock concerto, and I wanted it to totally encompass the audience with music from the heart. It worked out that way, too. For when I first conducted it, I looked out into the audience during the third movement and they were tapping their feet, smiling and clapping their hands—even the older people.

As a performer, the greatest enjoyment also comes from pleasing people and seeing them respond. And the funny experiences of my career come during performances. On one occasion, while I was still a child of five, I was giving a concert for the patients of a veterans' hospital. They only had one room large enough and they put the piano in the center of a highly polished ballroom floor without bracing the piano legs. When I started on a fast section of my first piece, the piano, which had casters on its legs, started rolling away from me. I leaned forward and it kept rolling. I tried to hook my foot around a piano leg but it kept on. So I stood up and kept playing, following the piano around the room as it rolled. The veterans certainly liked that performance, and I'll never forget it.

For girls interested in music, I'd like to pass on some advice I received as a child. I had the honor of meeting a lady I greatly admired, Dame Myra Hess, one of the foremost pianists of her generation. "Remember one thing," she said, "if you practice fifteen minutes a day and you totally concentrate on what you're doing, that is the equivalent of just sitting there and practicing for four hours while daydreaming about other things."

Myself, I'd tell girls to have a goal, a dream, to find out what you want to do in life, and do whatever it is to the best of your ability. Be prepared to hear the word no a lot. As long as you've worked hard and know you're qualified, you should never take a no to heart, but just keep trying. If you really find that you aren't right in one musical niche, however, don't be afraid to try another. There are many roles for a musician: performing, coaching, teaching, arranging, composing, editing, scoring films and more.

Discipline is perhaps hardest and most important—important to have, and important not to have too much of. Have the discipline to avoid such things as drugs; they can't take away your problems. Face your problems, because they'll always be waiting there for you until you do. Have the discipline to work when you need to, even though there are times you'd rather do something else. But don't let discipline take over your life. If you become a perfectionist and automaton, the heart will go out of you. You can't live your work, you must live your life.

Jeanne Morris SPORTSWRITER

Most of the sports I learned to like as a girl, I learned about from my mother who was a sports nut. I can remember one Saturday, when we lived in California, there were three big games the same day. My mother, my sister and I didn't want to miss any of them, so mom listened to one in the kitchen, my sister sat by the radio in the living room, and I turned on the car radio in the garage. We left all the doors open and shouted the scores to one another whenever they changed.

I'm still a sports nut, and now I have a job where I can use what I know. When I got my first job as a sports reporter, I had not heard of another woman in the field, but now I hear of more and more every day. It's not a closed field.

My first job was with a newspaper. Although I hadn't studied journalism, I'd always been a compulsive writer. While my four children were small, I wrote stories, articles and sample newspaper columns at home. A friend gave one of these sample columns to a newspaper that was looking for a sportswriter, and they hired me to write about sports for the women's pages, then gave me a column in the sports pages. I also do sports interviews on TV, and articles for magazines occasionally.

Mostly, I do feature writing, that is, stories about sports rather than scores or outlines of the games. The subject of sports is rich in unused stories. It gives me an unusual opportunity to bring out the human side of an athlete's personality, to bring out the human interest angles in an event.

There are sports where the atmosphere and the characters involved make fascinating reading in themselves. Two of the most interesting people I've met, for example, are in boxing. In a sport like that you meet people whose game is their whole world, whose whole identity is tied up in the gym, and all their conversation centered around it. The famous sports journalists Red Smith and Damon Runyan were great because they didn't write so much about the sports as about the people in them, and the charm and the traditions that surrounded them. I hope sports don't get so businesslike that these things are lost.

Another thing I enjoy about sports reporting and just plain

watching is the beauty of the games. Track, for example, is a beautiful thing. It's the only pure sport: just yourself against your own body. There's beauty in football, too—like watching how Gale Sayers ran. When he carried the football, he seemed to have eyes in back of his head, and moved in the most extraordinary way.

So far, the biggest difficulty for me has been interviewing basketball players on TV. I'm so short, and they're so tall, that the only way we can use the same microphone is for me to stand on a very big box.

One of the most rewarding projects I've worked on was a book about Brian Piccolo, a young football player who died recently of cancer. I originally started doing tape recorded interviews with Brian about his life and his career, just to keep him busy during his illness. When he died, I decided to make the tapes into a book, so that his daughters, who were very young at the time, would know what he was like and have an image of him.

One of the things that concerns me now is that there are so few sports programs for girls in the schools. I'm working to change that, and also to help inner city kids get more consideration in college sports recruiting. As it is now, they get passed up too often.

Sometimes I hear a girl say that she would like to work for a news magazine but doesn't think she can get with one, so she'll settle for whatever comes along. Or that she thinks a woman can only work for a ladies magazine so she'll only apply there. I hate to see a girl quit before she starts. Whenever I talk to girls who are studying journalism, I try to let them know that they shouldn't be put off by competition, and settle for something they don't really want. You can do your best work (and the most good) writing about a subject you love.

Sharon Harris DRESS DESIGNER

As far back as I can remember I loved to sew—dolls, aprons, dresses and ruffles. Ruffles and more ruffles, for hours at a time. When I was ten I made a sailor dress I was very proud of, and at Christmas I'd earn money making dolls and dresses for my friends and neighbors. So there I was, a small businesswoman already, and yet it didn't occur to me that I could make a career of what I enjoyed most.

Instead, I went to art school, then switched schools to study political science. When graduation from college came, I still didn't know what I wanted to do, but I did know I needed a new wardrobe to go job hunting. Everything I found that I liked was too expensive, so I set to work designing new clothes for myself. The results surprised me. They were better than some I'd seen in the stores. So I went to the manager and buyer of a local department store. Not only did she encourage me, but ordered several of each of my designs in several different sizes. Suddenly I was really in business. I quickly signed up for courses in pattern making and sizing and learned much of the business as I went along.

Of course, this is an unusual way to break into the business. Most designers study formally in an art school or professional school, and then apprentice with an established designer or look for work as a designer with a manufacturer of clothing.

After being on my own for a while, I decided to take a job designing for a manufacturer of women's clothing. Generally, a manufacturer does not allow a new designer to have his or her name on the clothing labels. But I was allowed to have my name on the labels from the start since I had already established my name in the work I had done on my own.

Much of my inspiration comes from my friends and from people on the streets rather than from history of fashion, books or movies. I like to design for actively involved women. They need clothes that they can wear to meetings or to work and then possibly to dinner or a party afterward. In other words, they need adaptable clothes that can be worn many different ways. I adapt many of the latest trends to fit the lives of my friends and myself.

Often when my company sends me on a trip to Europe for

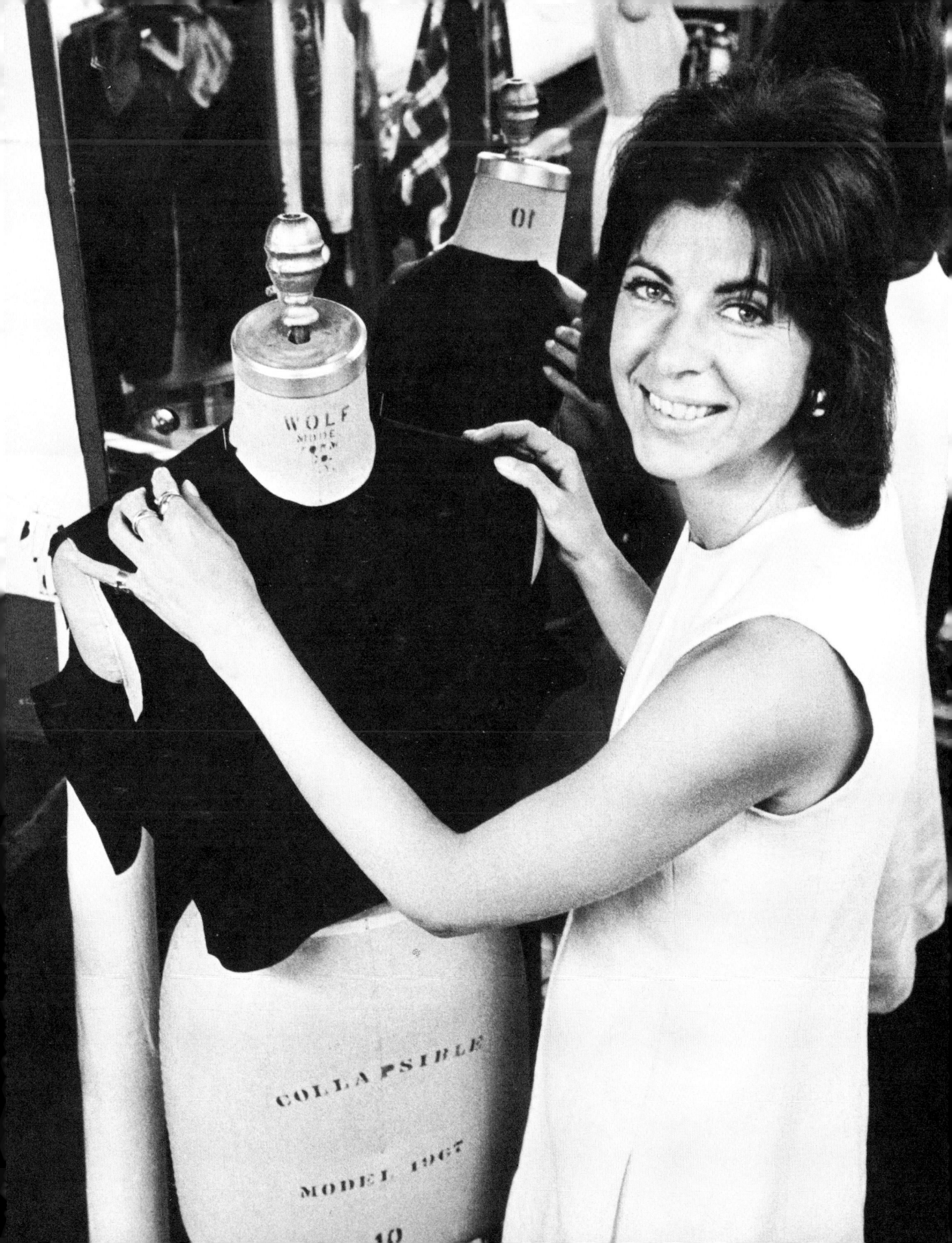

inspiration, I go not to see the showings of famous designers, but to watch the people in the streets. Especially the young people who haven't much money for clothes and who make their own, setting their own fashions. Lately I haven't needed to travel much to Europe, because the inspiration for the main trends in fashion has been coming from America.

When I visit Europe I often shop for fabric, as I do here. Often the inspiration for a design will come from the fabric itself. A particularly beautiful cloth, by its texture, color, pattern or drape, may suggest ideas for a dress or suit that will show off the fabric's attractive qualities.

My methods are much different now from the days when I did all of the work myself. Now I make sketches, order fabric, and decide how many of each design to make. Then the design goes to a patternmaker, the pattern goes to a cutter, the cut fabric pieces are given to a seamstress, the sewn garments are given to pressers, the pressed garments are given to salespeople and shippers who get them to the stores which sell them.

Clothes are bought by the stores at the beginning of each season, so we must have them ready by certain dates, five times a year—a show for each season and one of transitional clothes. The showings are held either in a hotel or our New York showroom. When deadlines get near, there's a lot of pressure. Buyers for the stores are invited, the showroom is filled, and models appear wearing each design. Up until then I've been working hard, seeing the designs up close only, and wondering if they will be well received. When the clothes finally appear at the showings, they always do look good to me.

There are other satisfactions too. My first big award was a thrill, and so was seeing my name on the labels of my designs for the first time. I always get a good feeling from seeing someone walking down the street in a dress I recognize as one of my designs. And there's still the fun I remember having as a girl of seeing real clothes come to life from sketches.

Ellen Lanyon PAINTER

Being an artist is not something one can pass a test and be given a license for, but a way of thinking that one grows into. This happens as you develop the strength to see yourself as an artist, to work alone on your own initiative, and by learning to see the world about you as an artist does.

Several things helped me to develop the ego I needed to say, "I am an artist," and the drive I had to have to keep working year after year.

The first was the encouragement I got from teachers, friends and family when I did well in my early school art classes. In addition, both my grandfathers were painters. One was a buggy striper. In his day people rode in buggies, not cars, and those buggies were elaborately decorated by painters. The other grandfather was a decorator of houses, which at that time meant painting large areas of home interiors with garlands, cupids, flowers and scrolls. He also did many watercolors and oil paintings. When this grandfather died, I was twelve years old, and my parents saw to it that I inherited his painting equipment. They cleaned the brushes and palettes, wrapped everything up and presented it to me. They had been very proud of him, and I felt that they were proud of me, too.

The second help was in learning to *see* as an artist: to really start looking and to use my eyes. I got a scholarship to an art museum school and would roam the galleries during lunch hour, thinking about what it means to create a new image and interpret life. There's always a new way to interpret—you can never feel that everything has been done. I began collecting objects as most artists do. I would keep those things that attracted me visually. My studio is cluttered with old post cards, mirrors, jumping jacks, fans and such things. I live with them for a while, study them and put them into my work. A toy may sit in my studio for months, because something about its form attracts me, and then eventually I will begin to draw it, paint it, and absorb it into my work, either as it is or just in essence.

The third, and most helpful thing, was my study at a professional art school. I preferred it to a university or college, because I was already sure of what I wanted to do. I lived at home, rather than on a campus, so I wasn't in a social situation. And I had a job after school. I think it made me grow up faster. One teacher in particular helped me believe in myself as an artist. He told us there was really no big difference between students and painters, and he got us a show. Another great teacher, who we called Miss Van, helped even more. She encouraged individual work, helping us to be more independent. But it was at a summer art school, Oxbow, that I got the greatest feeling of what it means to be a dedicated creative person. I had been babysitting for the daughter of two painters who had both worked there and they encouraged me to go. I got a work scholarship which enabled me to study there. At Oxbow I could work, produce, and be associated with professional people. I learned to think of my painting as something I did daily, like a job, even though it's done at home.

While I was still working on my degree at the Art Institute, several of us students began exhibiting as a group. As I exhibited more and my name became known, a gallery in Chicago and another in New York agreed to sell my work. This is extremely helpful for an artist, to have a gallery handle her work. The galleries have exhibitions of my paintings and prints each year. In addition I have one-woman shows elsewhere and exhibit in many group shows.

When I graduated from school my parents thought I should become a commercial artist and begin to make a living. They worried that I would not be able to support myself by just painting. But I went on in school and got a master's degree so that I could teach college art courses and continue with my own work. It's true that an artist can never depend on making the same kind of money that people do in some other professions. But when you accept art or teaching as a profession, you know that the rewards are such that it exceeds the money.

When I married and had children I arranged my life so that I could paint, and had a studio in my home. At first I would work only when the children were asleep, but I found more and more time as they grew older. It helps that my husband is also a painter and university professor. Sometimes we get grants which are like awards for achievement in the form of enough money to live on

for as much as a year. They are given by foundations and they free you to paint full time, travel or study. When my husband got a grant to travel and paint in Rome for a year, I went along with him, and when I got a grant for study at the University of London, he went along with me. Later we were able to travel with our children to Italy and Greece. This open, informal kind of life, with both parents working at home much of the time, is an interesting one for our children. They are so used to it that they don't think about it, but they like it and it is a little different than their friends' homes. Their friends like to come and visit.

    The subject matter in my work has changed through the years, but I usually paint figures, objects, and scenes that can be identified, rather than abstract works. At first I painted cityscapes, then interiors I remembered from my childhood. Then I discovered old photographs from family albums and tried to capture the quality they had—the patterns of strong light and shadow and the nostalgia for long-gone family activities. For a while I was drawn to sports themes and did paintings of action. One of my latest themes is magic. I began collecting old magic-trick catalogues, and visiting a neighbor who is a magician. He builds stage equipment for magic tricks. The magic works depict props such as the boxes through which the magician pulls silk scarves that turn into other things, like rabbits coming from hats. Now I am getting away from the magic themes to create my own original fantasies on canvas.

    I find that if I am away from my work for a while, I get out of sorts—it's actually something that I need and must do. And I feel I can make a contribution by my work, to the time I live in and to my social environment, by documenting life around me. I feel that the most exciting thing about art is that an artist can create new ways of looking at things and influence people into seeing things a little differently. She can change attitudes, give people new visions, and make them notice things. An artist has a great deal of power.

June Pykacek THEATER DIRECTOR

The two things I wanted to be most as a child were things that there was little opportunity to practice. I wanted to be both a trapeze artist and an actress. Being a trapeze artist meant joining the circus, and my parents didn't care for that idea. Being an actress meant having plays to act in. And although there were occasional plays done in my school or in summer camp, it wasn't quite enough. I began staging my own productions. At any opportunity, I'd get neighborhood children together and put on my own plays. Sometimes we couldn't find an audience of more than one, but we had fun performing even for that one. When an opportunity such as a birthday party gave me a larger audience, I'd put together as big a production as I could, complete with costumes and scenery. I'm not sure my friends always enjoyed being captive audiences at my birthday parties, but I certainly enjoyed these plays. In particular I remember a melodrama I put together for my fourteenth birthday when I gave myself the role of the villain, dressed in one of my father's old coats.

I studied acting and theater in college, in a theater school in Chicago, and with an acting coach in New York. But I was dissatisfied with acting, because as an actress I could not be the one to decide which plays were to be performed. Even if I could get the best roles available, those might still be roles in plays I disliked. The kind of play that really interested me was not being done. I liked modern, experimental, lively and imaginative plays, and the ones being done were older, more traditional types.

I can't get excited about doing traditional plays, since I don't share the feelings those plays express; they speak of old wars and old times that I haven't known. Today's wars and today's problems are my experience and I seek out plays about them. Two of my favorite contemporary playwrights are Jean-Claude Vonitallie and Maria Irene Fornes.

Although I like seeing and putting on new plays, I still love reading classics and learning from them. I still find Shakespeare exciting and I enjoy George Bernard Shaw's plays because of the women's roles in them. They are interesting, independent women, every bit as important to Shaw's plays as the male roles.

Since my strongest interest was in the plays themselves, it was natural for me to give up acting in favor of directing. As a director I could choose my plays, as long as I could find a producer or theater to let me do them.

The usual way of getting a start as a director is to gain as much experience as possible in college and community theater, repertory companies and whatever else is available. Those interested in directing films often migrate to Hollywood, those interested in theater to New York. They then look for theaters and producers interested in the plays they want to do. Once their reputations are established, they are sought out by producers and theaters.

When I started out as a director, however, new, experimental plays were not being done. So I started my own theaters, wherever I happened to be. Most of these were in the Chicago area, which gave me a potentially large audience.

My first job as a director is to choose the play. I read a great many plays, usually choose new and unusual ones that have something to say. Sometimes a play looks like fun to do, but the author hasn't much to say. You can make the play mean something more than the author intended by adding, changing, or dressing up the play with various stage effects. The author may either be grateful for your resourcefulness or very angry with you for meddling with the original.

Once a play is chosen, I set up the date of its opening, determine the length of the rehearsal period, and choose the actors and actresses. A casting call is announced and those who would like to be in the play show up to try out for various parts.

Casting a play is like working a puzzle. A playwright usually gives a general description of each character at the beginning of the play. The actors and actresses chosen must fit those descriptions, but also must have the qualities of temperament that suit them for the parts. Each play has a certain style; some actors and actresses are in tune with it and some aren't. Each person chosen must be right for his or her part, and each of these people complement one another in their roles.

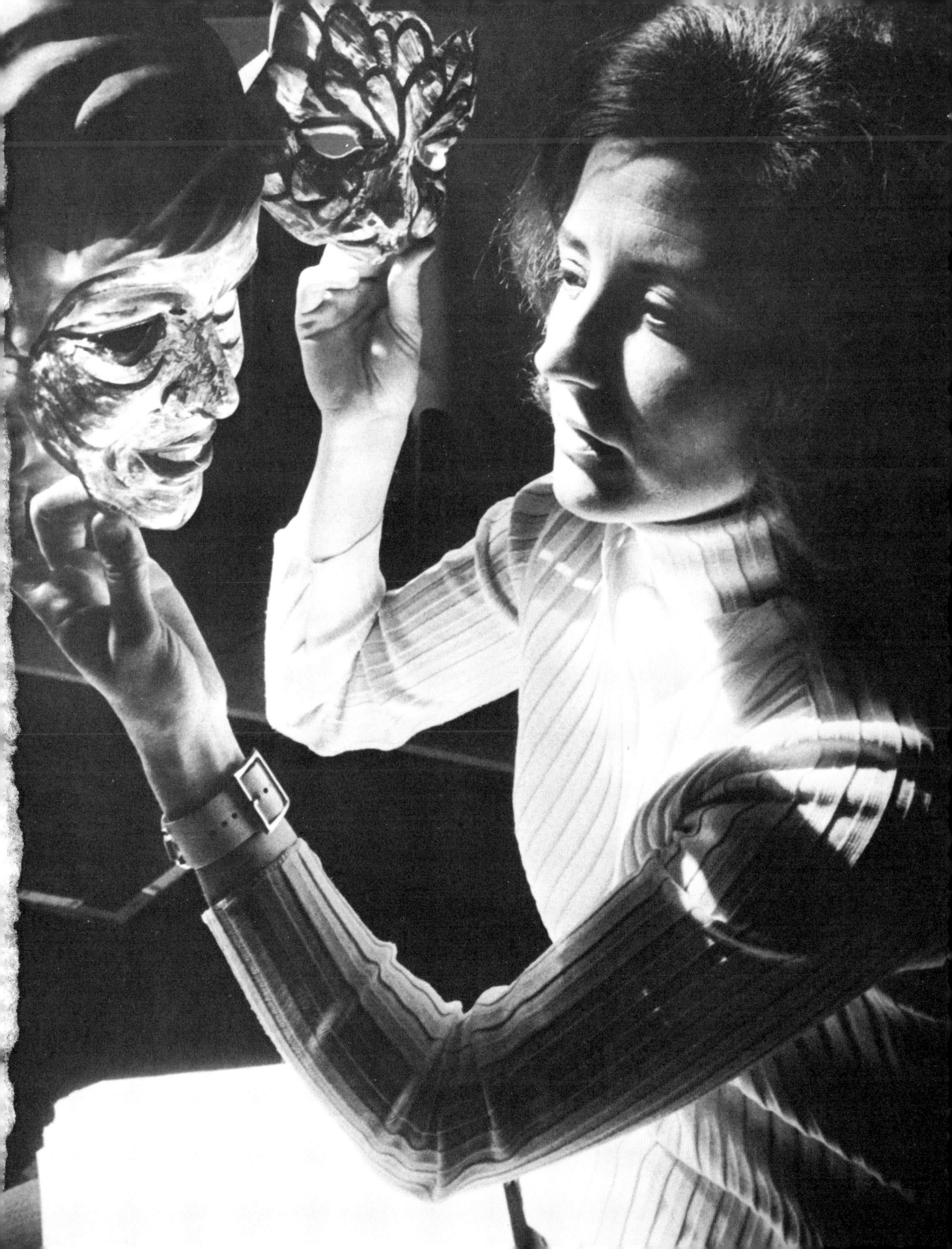

Then I interpret the play to express the author's meaning. I discuss the play with actors I've chosen and help them understand who their characters are, what the characters lives are like, what each character wants within the action of the play, and how to go about showing this. At each point in the play, even if a character has no lines, the person playing the role should know why the character is there.

I help actors and actresses use their own personalities to express the qualities of the roles they play. In a play I'm doing now, a group of characters appear who are frivolous, vain, charming, empty and wrapped up in their own little social world. They move about among one another, and every once in a while, they all freeze, holding postures that express their vanity. The scene has a dance-like feeling—a vanity dance. To find the right postures, I suggested to the cast that they each look into a mirror and see what sort of postures they would assume—what sort of little gestures and poses a person might fall into in trying to look more beautiful, or showing off his or her best features. I told them to concentrate on their *own* best features. They then used their own little vanities as their character's vanities.

Between rehearsals, I work with the set designer to plan scenery that will convey the mood of the play and the place in which the action occurs. I talk to the lighting person to help plan the stage lighting that will help establish this mood and a prop person who finds the objects the cast will use on stage. I also must concern myself with sound and music. I talk to the sound person, who is skilled in sound effects, and the musical director or conductor and musicians if there is music in the show. I let them know where sounds and music occur and how they fit into the play; then they rehearse with the cast.

A director must coordinate all these separate theatrical elements to make a unified production that brings to life what the playwright intended to say. In doing this, I like to let each person in the company make suggestions. I'm not an authoritarian director who likes giving orders. I enjoy getting the entire company to work together, each contributing something special.

It's usually great fun for me to work on a play, and most thrilling when it is finally on stage and my job is finished. To sit back and watch your finished work in performance is fascinating. The play now has a life of its own, but it is a life that you are familiar with because of all you have put into it. I'm so happy with some of the plays I've done I could watch them every night they're performed. Others I'm not as satisfied with.

Because they've been watching me direct plays since they were very young, my two children, who are eleven and twelve years old, are very helpful critics. They have an eye for what is happening onstage, and like to come to rehearsals. My daughter knows instinctively when someone is right or wrong for a part, and she usually shares her observations with me. My son loves to suggest stage business—movements actors might make as certain characters, or little things that might be added to make a play more interesting. In a comedy western I once did, he thought a spitting contest would be fun for the cowboys to engage in. I put it in the play and it was very funny.

A girl who is interested in theater can begin to explore the field by reading plays. She can do this even if the nearest theater is hundreds of miles away. Every library contains plays, and girls as young as fourteen can read and enjoy Shakespeare. A girl might also ask her parents to take her to the theater on special occasions, visit theater departments at nearby colleges, or take part in community theaters.

She should also know that theater is a competitive and overcrowded field. Top directors in New York may only do one or two plays a year. The same is true of film directors. There are many community theaters and larger repertory theaters throughout the country, however. But there will never be as many theaters as there are people who want to work in them. Theater will always be an overcrowded field simply because it is so much fun. If you love it, you just don't want to do anything else.

Mary Laney RADIO-TV REPORTER

Both of my parents had a great influence upon my life and choice of career. Without trying to pick out a career for me they helped me learn those things that led me to it.

My father always told me that an education was one of the greatest assets I could have, one that would always stay with me. He used to tell me that readers were leaders and encouraged me to read all I could. As a result, I've always kept up with the newspapers, faithfully read newsmagazines, and learned to really enjoy books, all of which have been an invaluable help to me in radio and television reporting.

Another thing my father repeated was that there was no reason to settle down and get married without getting a good start at life first. When my friends were rushing to get married he would tell me I'd be better off if I got my education and a start in my work first. It must have been good advice for me, since I love both my work and my husband.

My mother helped me in a much different way. I had a tremendous inferiority complex because I used to have a birthmark that covered the right side of my face. I used to come home crying because kids would say things like, "Don't play with her, you'll catch it." My mother would tell me the story, *The Ugly Duckling*, who grew up to be a beautiful swan. She often spent time reassuring me that I was not ugly, and that when the birthmark was removed I would grow away from these problems and become a beautiful swan.

So I refused to let the children's teasing make me shy. I decided I was going to be something. I knew I could make people listen, could write interesting things and be very funny. I learned to use these things to relate to people.

Reading, speaking and acting continued to interest me as I grew older. When I reached college, I felt I would like to major in speech and later get a law degree. I was attracted by the drama of the courtroom and participated in college debates whenever I could. But almost every year when I'd go to register for courses, the speech classes would be filled. I was also interested in history, so I filled in with history courses which proved to be valuable.

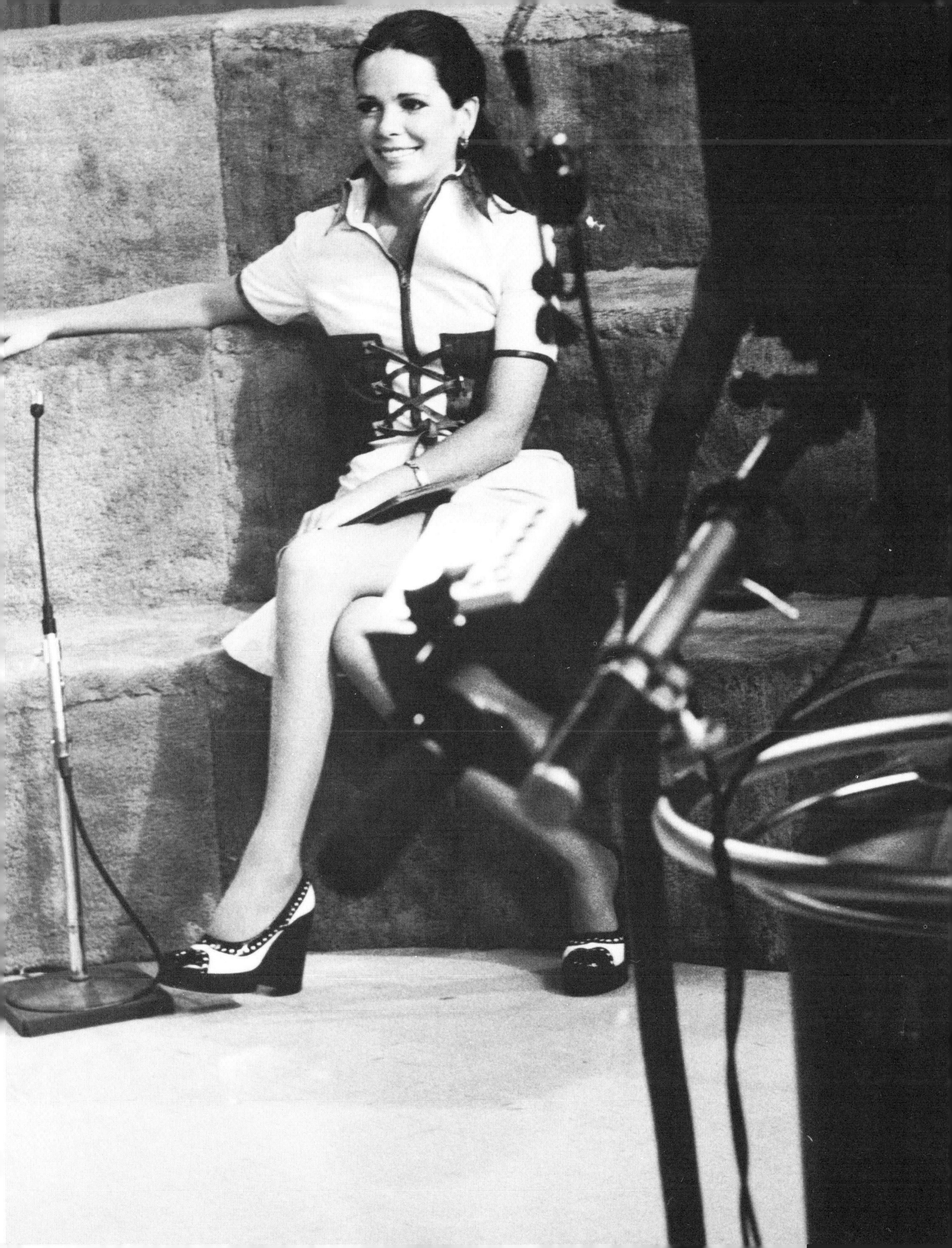

I also gained some job experience while in college, for I wanted very much to put myself through school. I had often heard my father talk of working his way through and wanted to show him I could do the same. I saved all the checks he sent me and instead of cashing them, I tied them up with a red ribbon and gave them back to him at Christmastime. Paying my own way seemed to make me work harder at my classes. I felt I got better grades than I would have if I hadn't been working.

I also took courses in political science, and one day my professor in that course asked me to help him with a research project. I went to the state capitol for him and began recording interviews with the political and government people I met there. It occurred to me that I was enjoying the interviewing more than writing, which had interested me most until then.

Following up this new interest, I went to a local television station and asked for a job. There were no women I knew of doing television interviewing then, but I didn't think that should keep me back.

The first job I was sent out on was to interview drivers in an auto race. The men there only saw women near the track when a driver had won a race and was being given flowers and a kiss of congratulation. The first driver I approached with my microphone must have thought that I was there to congratulate him, for he quickly took off his helmet and gave me a big kiss, while the TV cameras rolled on. I was quite flustered, but went on with the interview.

When I graduated I made a list of all the stations in a major city and got a job at the first one I went to. I told them that with my background in history I could not only bring out the news as it was presented that day, but also could point out what was happening at the same time in other countries and compare it with what happened ten years ago. In other words, I would cover the news in depth.

I had a little trouble getting ahead at first. My boss said that I shouldn't be on camera reading the news stories I wrote because people would resent hearing the news from someone so young and audiences would not believe a woman as they would a man. Times have changed since then, of course, and women are seen as newscasters on major stations. I'm very glad of this.

When applying for a reporter's job in radio, you bring along a demonstration tape of yourself reporting a news story. One way to prepare this is to find a story in the newspaper, rewrite it as you would report it, and read it onto a tape. For television a videotape is necessary—both picture and sound. If you don't have facilities to prepare this, you must ask the station to give you a videotape audition. In either case, the most important thing is to get an *in-person* interview, taking along your tape and a written résumé of your experience and education. It's also important to send a thank-you note to everyone you call on. When busy people give you their time, they'll remember it if you thank them.

The best way to prepare for such a job is to study, to read everything you can, and to keep up with the news. It helps to pick a few new words from the dictionary each day and learn them. In technical areas, such as operating camera equipment, it's necessary to have specialized radio-television courses. But for a reporter's job, this is not the case. It's best to study whatever field interests you most. For example, if you are interested in education, study that and you can specialize in reporting on education. A lawyer-reporter would be best at reporting what is happening in a courtroom because he or she really understands it. All the media are becoming specialized in this way.

While I was still new in television reporting, I received some valuable advice from an older and very successful newscaster. He told me never to feel intimidated in a big-city station just because I was from a small town. Then he told me how many of the celebrities in our business came from small towns: it was quite a list and hardly any big names were left out.

As a matter of fact, it's not even necessary these days to go to a major city to get into the news media. News media all over the country are getting more and more sophisticated. And they are beginning to realize that everyone in the country is not interested only in what's happening in New York City. There is more news being reported from all over.

Then, too, there are more jobs besides those for writers and reporters in radio and television. Producing, directing, sales and technical jobs—working with camera, sound and other equipment.

It's true that this is a very competitive field. But I love competition and I work better with it. I've always felt that it was important to keep faith in something outside myself and to accomplish things for some purpose greater than myself. This kind of thinking helps you to compete only with yourself. You should not say, "There's another person applying for this job and I have to be better." You should think, "There's someone else trying for this job and I'm going to do my best."

Jackie Rivet   FILM MAKER

In college I was majoring in theater and very interested in acting. I did lots of little theater work and some television, including a children's television show which I produced and wrote.

After graduation, I went to Los Angeles, intending to break into acting. But when I saw the lifestyle of actors there I realized that world was not for me. When push came to shove, I wasn't confident in my abilities as an actress.

So I made a list of large cities where I might find film work of some kind, picked one by the process of elimination and arrived there with only forty dollars. Luckily I had one friend living there and borrowed her living room sofa to sleep on until I could get my own place.

I started making rounds of film studios looking for a job, but not knowing just where I'd fit in. One day a woman who interviewed me said, "You'd make a good assistant director." I wasn't even sure what that was, but accepted a job as assistant director in a large film studio where commercials and short films were made.

It was the hardest work I had done in my life, and the hours were the longest. Moreover, "assistant director" turned out to be a very unglamorous job. But I had found a field I wanted to know everything about and kept at it until I had.

The more I learned and the more I could do on my own, the more impatient I became with making commercials of the kind we did there. I began to feel that I was painting myself into a corner by working for a studio. I wanted to be my own person. So I began free-lancing—which means that I was my own company, working on one or two projects at a time.

I enjoyed the creative freedom of working for myself, but accepted many new responsibilities along with it. It's only a few steps from in front of the camera as an a actor, to behind the camera as a film maker, but there's a world of difference and years of learning in those few steps.

When I do a film or commercial, I'm the writer, producer and director all in one. I must hire a camera crew and actors and am responsible for paying them. A typical project goes like this:

First I, or a sales representative, go to call on companies, organizations and associations of all kinds. Any group that might need a commercial or film made at some time is a possible client. I show the work I have done in the past—a sample reel of film. If the group I'm calling on decides to give me a contract for a film, they become my client. They explain what the film will be for, and I propose ideas that will express what they have to say.

For example, if the film is to be on drug abuse, I think up ways to tell of this problem in words and pictures. To tell of it in a way that will reach people, make them think and make them want to act to solve the problem. If we agree on the concept, I begin writing a script. In the meantime, we must confer with lawyers, arrange details of our contract and make sure we have proper insurance.

Next I pre-produce. I get my camera crew together, all of them free-lancers, and confer with them on what equipment we will need to rent. I audition actors and choose those who are right for the film. A schedule is arranged and everyone is notified as to when they are needed.

Then comes the next role for me as director. During the actual filming I must work with the actors to communicate a set of feelings, and work with the camera crew on what kind of *visual* feeling I want to see created.

Once the film is completely shot, the crew wrapped, we send the film to the lab. It's developed, and a work print is made from it for editing. First the bad stuff (outtakes) is weeded out. Then we puzzle the pieces together to get flow, rhythm and pacing —elements that give a film dramatic impact. Those little magic moments the actors give us are set off to their best advantage. Movies are often really *made* in the editing process.

The finished film is put in a can—the concept we started with and all the work done since is contained in one small flat can.

I enjoy seeing the work when it's finished, but most of all I enjoy the challenge of making a film, creating the concept and carrying it out.

It also makes me happy that I'm able to give people jobs,

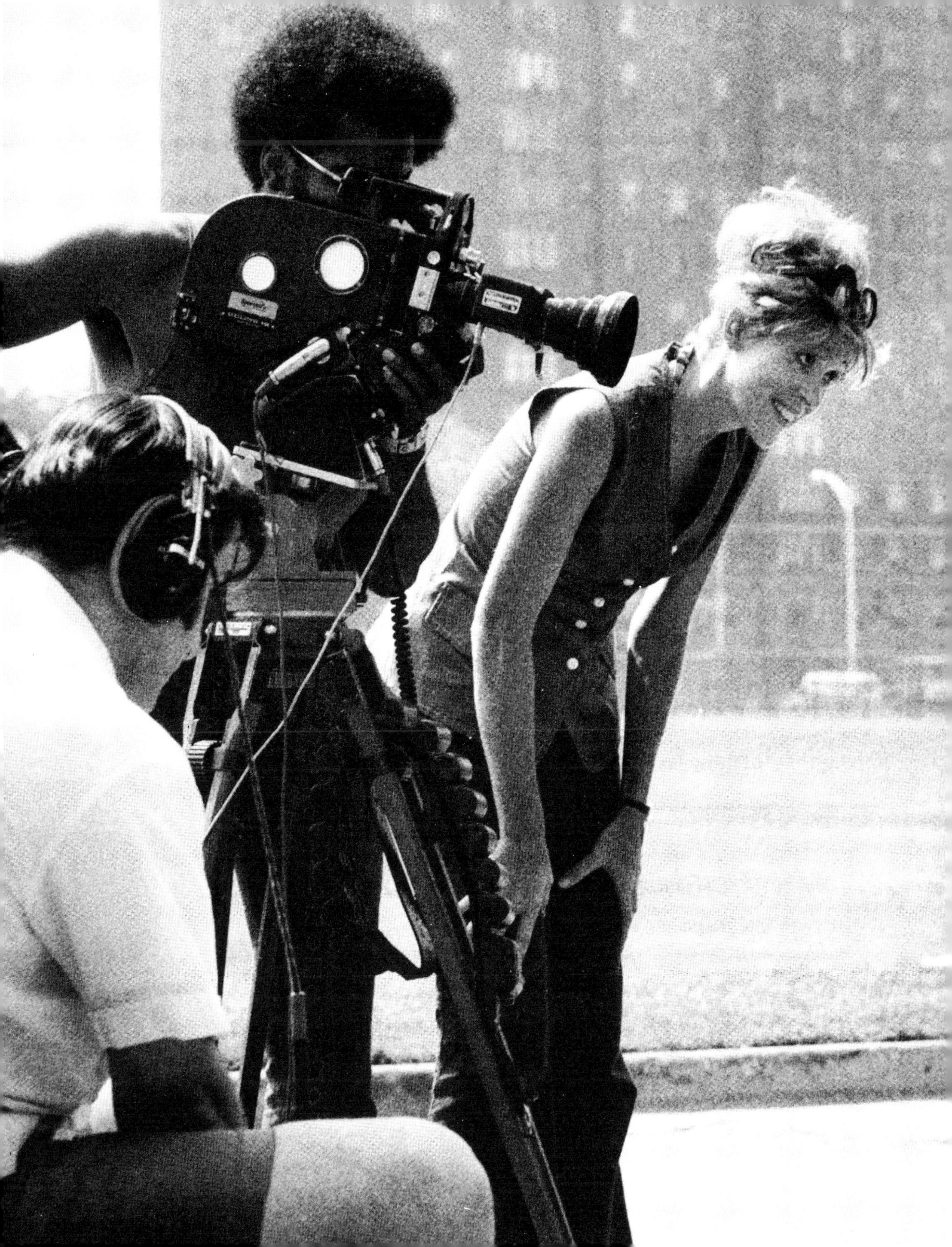

especially talented people who are having a hard time breaking into the business. I enjoy teaching, helping and watching people grow in their work.

When I was in school there were few schools with cinema departments, so I learned mostly on the job. These days one can study film in many schools, but on-the-job training is still very valuable.

I find film to be an exciting field. To be able to say something and to say it in an art form as well—this is a real balancing act, and I love it. In working hard to get the effects they want, however, some directors take themselves too seriously and hurt the people they are working with unnecessarily. So far I've always tried to put people first. If I started to take my work so seriously that it stopped being fun, I'd quit.

Irene Dailey   ACTRESS

As a child, I saw myself as the only ungifted member of a gifted family. I searched within myself for *my* special talent, for I was jealous of the attention given to my talented brother and sister.

Eventually I decided that I would be a writer, for I enjoyed creating characters. I wrote whenever possible in school and thought I'd found my field.

One day a friend was going to try out for a part in a small theater company's play. She asked me to come along and encouraged me to audition for a part too. It happened that I got the part she had come to the audition for.

I found that I really loved acting and began to be seriously interested in it. My parents didn't approve, but they didn't stop me either. Then followed several other parts in summer stock and small theater companies. I was beginning to build a career for myself, but was dissatisfied with my own work. I felt that I needed more training in my profession.

So I began to really study acting, movement and voice. I found my own values. I realized that I was an artist and wanted to practice the art of acting beautifully. I felt that I'd never know enough and that acting was a constant challenge.

Training is very important to me as an actress. A famous teacher of acting, Stanislavsky, once said that actors, like musicians, have scales they must practice. However, the instrument of the actor is that actor's own voice and body. Because I've trained myself to consciously control my muscles, I can relax them at will and avoid stage fright.

But acting is not done with only the body. The mind has a lot to do with it. People often ask me how I can appear in a play night after night, cry every time on cue, and do everything exactly the same way each time. My answer is that I never do everything exactly the same way each time, because each time seems like the first time. I have learned to "do it again for the first time" by believing in the circumstances of the play. If you believe in what is happening to the character you play, each time is the first time.

As a person, I often find I'm not able to express what I feel when I'm feeling it. There are times when I cannot cry. But on stage I can always cry when I'm supposed to, and I feel that my emotions have fuller expression there than they do in real life.

There are some technical differences to acting when it's in such different areas as stage, film and television, but I have worked in each of these mediums and the task of creating a character is the same in each case. For that's what acting is—creating a character. It's the very thing that I enjoyed most about writing when I wanted to be a writer.

Acting as a profession has its bleak moments; it's an insecure business and you never know which job comes next if at all. There are funny moments too. In one play I acted in, there is an argument between father and son about religion. One lady in the audience took this scene to heart so much that she forgot it was only a play and came up to the stage to join in the argument. In another play, a dog from one of the actor's dressing rooms came wandering down and onto the stage.

After several long years of theater apprenticeship, study, college drama, community theater and roles in many productions, I was an "overnight success" in a London play. After that I worked rather regularly as an actress on Broadway, in major films and on television.

But I still had a need for an extra dimension in my work and I found it in teaching. For several years I have been the artistic director and a teacher at the School of the Actors' Company. It's a new kind of school, for all the teachers are actors themselves. There are times when I enjoy teaching even more than acting. And I often learn through teaching.

The advice I most often give the young people I teach is that they should test their desire to become actors. It's an insecure profession and one I tell them they should not go into if there is anything else they can do as well or better. If anyone can talk you out of it, quit. If you love acting and *no one* can talk you out of it, if it's the only thing you can do well or the only thing you want to do, then it's right for you to try.

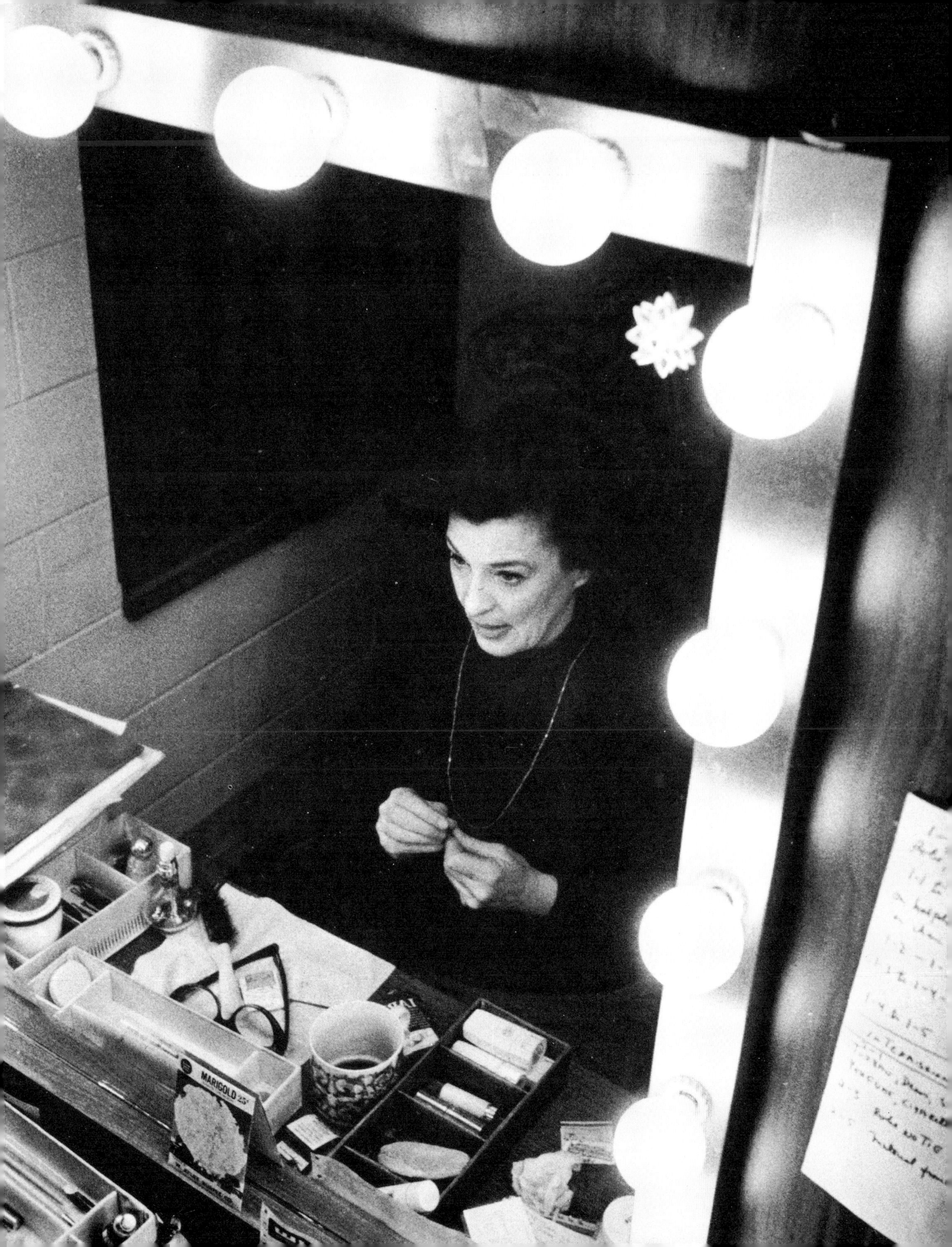
MARIGOLD 25¢

Lois Axeman ILLUSTRATOR

When I was six years old, drawing was my favorite pastime, and I still enjoy it as much now as then. There was always encouragement from my teachers, and I drew on everything I could, including my themes in school. I liked to illustrate them with pictures.

So I went on to art school and studied drawing, painting, illustration and design. While I was there, I sold my first work—a fashion illustration. Since I'd never done a commercial job before, I wasn't sure just what was expected. I took the dress home that I was to illustrate, drew it on a figure as I thought it should look, and the art director at the store seemed happy with it. It was printed in a newspaper ad and I remember buying several copies.

By the time I graduated I knew more of how one manages the business part of illustration, and as I got jobs I learned more of what various clients expected of me. First I got my portfolio together: I put samples of my work from school together with printed samples of commercial jobs I had done into a carrying case. Taking this along, I called on editors and art directors in every field I knew of where illustration was used, and showed them my work.

I decided from the start to free-lance rather than work for one particular studio. By free-lancing, I could work for many different clients, doing one particular job at a time and working in my own studio or at home.

I did fashion illustrations for department stores, children's book illustration for book publishers, story illustration for magazine publishers and jobs for design studios and advertising agencies.

As I tried various fields, I gradually found that the work I enjoyed most was illustrating children's books, so I began to specialize in that. I found an agent who would represent me, and he made calls with my portfolio and got me work in this field. Children's books call for illustrations full of imagination, bright colors, and figures full of action, and I enjoy that.

When I am given a job, the art director explains what is needed: whether the illustration should be in black and white or color, how many colors, what size it should be, whether the picture

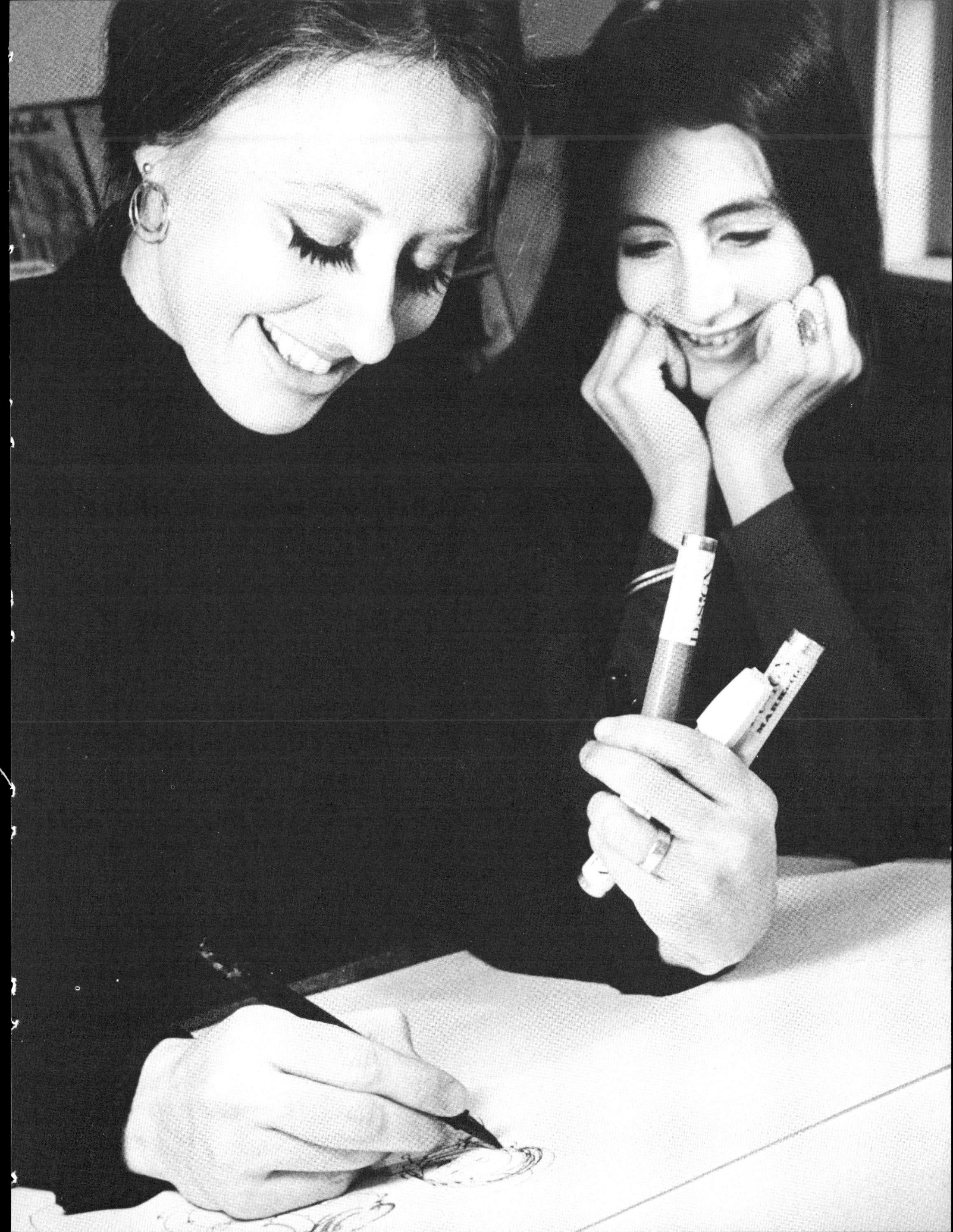

is to extend over one or several pages, how soon it is needed, et cetera. I use many different materials, from watercolors and marking pens to thin adhesive plastic that I cut into whatever shapes I want and attach to the picture as I work on it.

Recently my daughter has been doing many things I remember from my own schooldays: getting encouragement from teachers, winning prizes in school exhibits and drawing on everything. She was very proud to get her first job from her father, who is a designer, and to get paid for it, too.

I often think of how pleasant it is to do something for a living that I did as a child for fun. It's like being a grownup and a kid at the same time.

SCIENCE
& MEDICINE

Lynne Carlson VETERINARIAN

There are three main types of veterinary medicine and I was lucky to be exposed to all three as a child. In small animal practice, a veterinarian cares mainly for pets. An equine practice consists of racehorses and horse breeding farms. And a large animal practice includes cattle and large farm animals. I got to know all three because my parents had a farm on which they bred horses. Later they began breeding and selling dogs. And when they bought a new farm that had been a dairy farm, my mother decided it should be a dairy farm again and she bought a herd of cows.

Our veterinarian was a close friend of the family, but when he came to treat sick animals, my mother wouldn't allow us children to watch, since sick animals are not on their best behavior, and she was afraid we'd be hurt. Since I wasn't able to see the doctor make the animals well, what he did had an element of mystery. I wanted to be able to do such things too, and would tell anyone who asked that I wanted to be a veterinarian.

I would go to the veterinary clinic on Saturdays and help out, just to be around. As I got older, I was able to work there in the summers as a helper—getting things ready for surgery, cleaning kennels and working as a receptionist. As I learned more about veterinary medicine, I was as sure as ever that I wanted to study it, so I took all the science courses I could in high school. During my junior year my parents helped me look for a college. I went to visit one in my home state first, but the man who interviewed me there tried to discourage me. He didn't think women should try to be veterinarians because he felt no one would hire them. This was nonsense, but I didn't bother to fight him since I thought that a school which allowed such an attitude in its staff would be a terrible place to study. The next school I inquired at had an entirely different outlook. I was told that everything depended on my grades in the first year of school—so I made sure they were good. Just recently, I heard that the first school was in trouble for its bad attitude toward women. The federal government is threatening to stop giving the school government funds if it doesn't stop its discrimination.

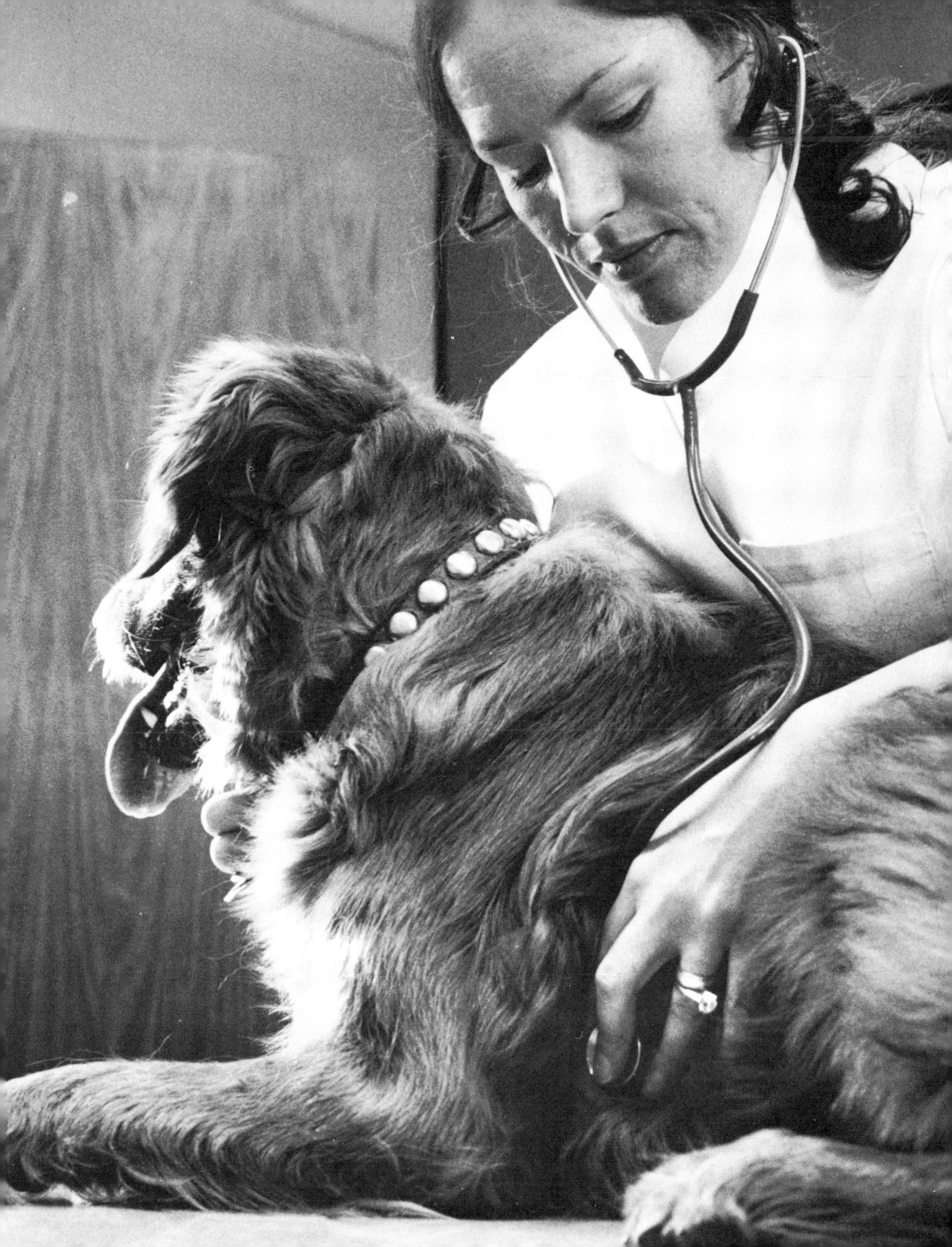

As I studied, I remained as interested in animals as before, but I became even more interested in medicine. I wanted to specialize in surgery, and found that in small animal practice I could use the more advanced and complicated surgical techniques I was learning. So that's what I chose for my special field.

After graduation, I soon found a place with a veterinary clinic. There were several other veterinarians on the staff and we worked from eight to six, and took our turns being on call for emergencies. When my daughter was born, I began to limit my work to special surgery for a while. This allowed me to work at prearranged times, and also let me do only the work that interested me most of all.

Some people have shown surprise when they see that the doctor is a woman, but when I start working with their animals and they see I know what I am doing, they have confidence in me. In a clinic, it is gratifying to know that sometimes people request that I be the one to take care of their pets.

There are some special considerations in working with animals. Just like a baby doctor, you are working with something that cannot tell you how it feels. You have to rely on signs of illness and laboratory tests. A sick animal is not going to be itself, and when it finds itself in strange surroundings at the veterinary clinic it will be afraid. If you have an abrupt manner, you will turn that animal's nervousness into defensive biting. I would never think of approaching an animal without speaking to it. Though they don't understand the words, animals can tell by the tone of your voice how you feel about them, and whether you want to help or harm them. You must also know how to interpret an animal's behavior. They give you signs, too. There are very few dogs that won't growl before they try to bite, for example. And a person who is afraid of animals is going to get bitten more often than someone who is not. These things must be learned by experience.

Another consideration is that there are times when an animal simply won't sit still for anyone. In veterinary school, you are taught how to hold an animal while you treat it. Often this is something your assistants must do for you because you need both hands for treatment. The veterinarian is there primarily for treatment, not restraint, after all. Therefore size and strength are not necessary in the doctor, even for the treatment of large animals. A friend of mine has an equine practice at a racetrack, and she is only five feet tall. For dairy cattle, there are special stocks in which an animal can be held for treatment.

There are many satisfactions in my work; the greatest is simply being able to relieve pain and help an animal recover from illness or injury. Especially in cases of serious injury, it is good to know you've made a big difference. I remember one case that seemed almost impossible. A little dog named Ziggy had been bitten in the chest by a much larger dog, and had a large hole torn in his chest. He was quickly becoming infected and was very hurt and ill. It took slow and careful repair work to close the hole, and weeks of care until the infection was gone, but we were able to save him. Now when he comes in, he's as lively as before, and the only sign of the incident is a slight dent in his side.

Often I feel I'm helping the owner of the pet as much as the animal itself, for people can be very attached to their pets. It's very hard to tell people that their animal cannot be helped, and sometimes it's necessary to put an animal to sleep. That's difficult, but part of my work.

Sometimes animals can be very amusing. The funniest incident I can remember at the clinic was with a German shepherd. He poked his head into a Halloween pumpkin to get some candy and his head stuck, giving him a pumpkin face. We had to use pliers to cut it off. He seemed so embarrassed and so sheepish—as though he had really been caught in the act.

Being a vet helped me in one way I didn't expect. After so much experience holding and handling small animals, and watching out for several things at once as I held them, I found that I had no problem getting used to holding a baby when I became a mother. My own mother was amazed at how fast I learned to handle the baby naturally, and said, "You hold it as if it were your sixth instead of your first."

There are only eighteen schools in the country that teach

veterinary medicine. Usually, a high school counselor can help you find out which is closest to you or best for you. Most of these schools have a preveterinary course of two years, and a degree takes four more. At some, you can go to school year-round and finish the entire degree in four years. In addition to degrees in veterinary medicine, some of these schools teach animal technology, a two-year course. Those who complete this course are veterinary paramedics and assist the doctor not only in nursing, but in surgery and in other important ways.

One good way to learn if this is the field for you is to work at a veterinary clinic after school or in the summer. I remember a girl who worked at a clinic with me one summer who loved being with animals, but was afraid to watch surgery because she felt it might make her sick. Gradually her curiosity overcame her fear, and as she began to observe operations she found that it was so interesting she didn't think of being sick.

Another way to learn about the field is through your nearest veterinarian or veterinary school. Many vets have open house at their clinics from time to time, usually during Veterinary Week, to let people know more about the field. Many schools have visitations at their clinics called "Vet-A-Visit." I've known some veterinarians who will take a busload of children down to a college having one of these programs. You can write to the nearest veterinary college to find out if they have one.

The reason for these efforts to acquaint people with the field is that a great shortage of veterinarians is expected in the future, especially in equine or large animal practices. It's expected that there will be an even greater shortage of veterinarians than of doctors, so the schools are encouraging young people to go into the field.

Edith McKee GEOLOGIST

There's so much talk these days about what is relevant, but I can't think of anything more relevant to people than geology. Geology is the study of the earth, both the surface and subsurface, and of course, it's the earth we live on! Meteorology, the study of the gas envelope which is our atmosphere, and geology, the study of the earth itself, are the fields which explain our environment. The particular environment of the planet earth is what enables us to live on it. Two of the most powerful tools for anyone who would be an environmentalist are geology and meteorology, for it takes scientific knowledge to know what can be done about environmental problems.

For example, the shape of a lake's basin and all the irregularities on the bottom of a lake determine how much water is in a lake and have a strong influence on the currents of that lake. These currents determine where pollutants will go. In Lake Michigan, if pollutants are put in the lake at Milwaukee or Chicago, we can predict exactly where those pollutants will travel from these cities, once we have basic information of how the currents run. With the same kind of information, we can tell where a pollutant has come from, no matter where it is found.

I became actively interested in measuring lake currents in 1966 when our country had lost an H-bomb off the coast of Spain, and a 727 plane had gone into Lake Michigan near Chicago. In both cases it was known where the plane and bomb had gone into the water, but because of currents, and the irregular shape of the lake and sea bottom, they could not be found where they fell in. It took two months in both cases for the objects to be found. I knew that the currents and bottoms of the Great Lakes and oceans should be mapped in detail and began a search for information and funds. I'm now completing such a project on Lake Michigan and have done some work in Lake Superior.

Most applications of geology are practical ones such as this. It helps in finding fuels, ores and water supplies. Geologists are needed to study the foundation conditions before buildings are put up, to determine if the ground beneath will support a building.

They also help in finding power sources—gas, oil, nuclear and electric—and in locating proper sites for the power plants.

One of my contributions to the field of geology has been the development of three-dimensional maps, called terrain diagrams, that make a dramatic presentation of technical exploration data, pulling together many technical details in a form anybody can understand. I first learned the value of graphic three-dimensional mapping during World War II when I was called out of the university to help interpret maps. My professors knew that I had some knowledge in this area and told me that geologists who could draw were needed to work with the military geology unit of the U.S. Geological Survey.

The problem was that although the army had magnificent detailed technical maps, these were so very technical that most of those who were fighting the war could not use them at all. We turned the technical information into maps in three dimensions, accurate enough to use for such wartime activities as bombing missions, finding landing sites and planning roads. World War II was a war that nearly everyone in the country had clear feelings about. We wanted to see Hitler and Nazism stopped. So I worked very hard to prepare these maps of Europe, North Africa and the Pacific theaters, using all sorts of field information. It was like crawling over the hills and valleys on my hands and knees. I became so familiar with the terrain, working in my office in Washington, that after the war was over and I visited some of these areas, I recognized them.

I've extended this mapping technique to underground exploration for ores and oil deposits that are hidden from the eye. Even if the oil deposits are 10,000 feet under the surface, they can be mapped with almost as much detail as what you might see in photos of the earth's surface taken from a plane. This is the technique I use also in my work of mapping lake and ocean bottoms.

While I have worked for big oil companies, I prefer working as a consultant, on a project by project basis, or proposing projects of my own and then raising the money for them. Sometimes the work involves routine exploration; sometimes it involves true

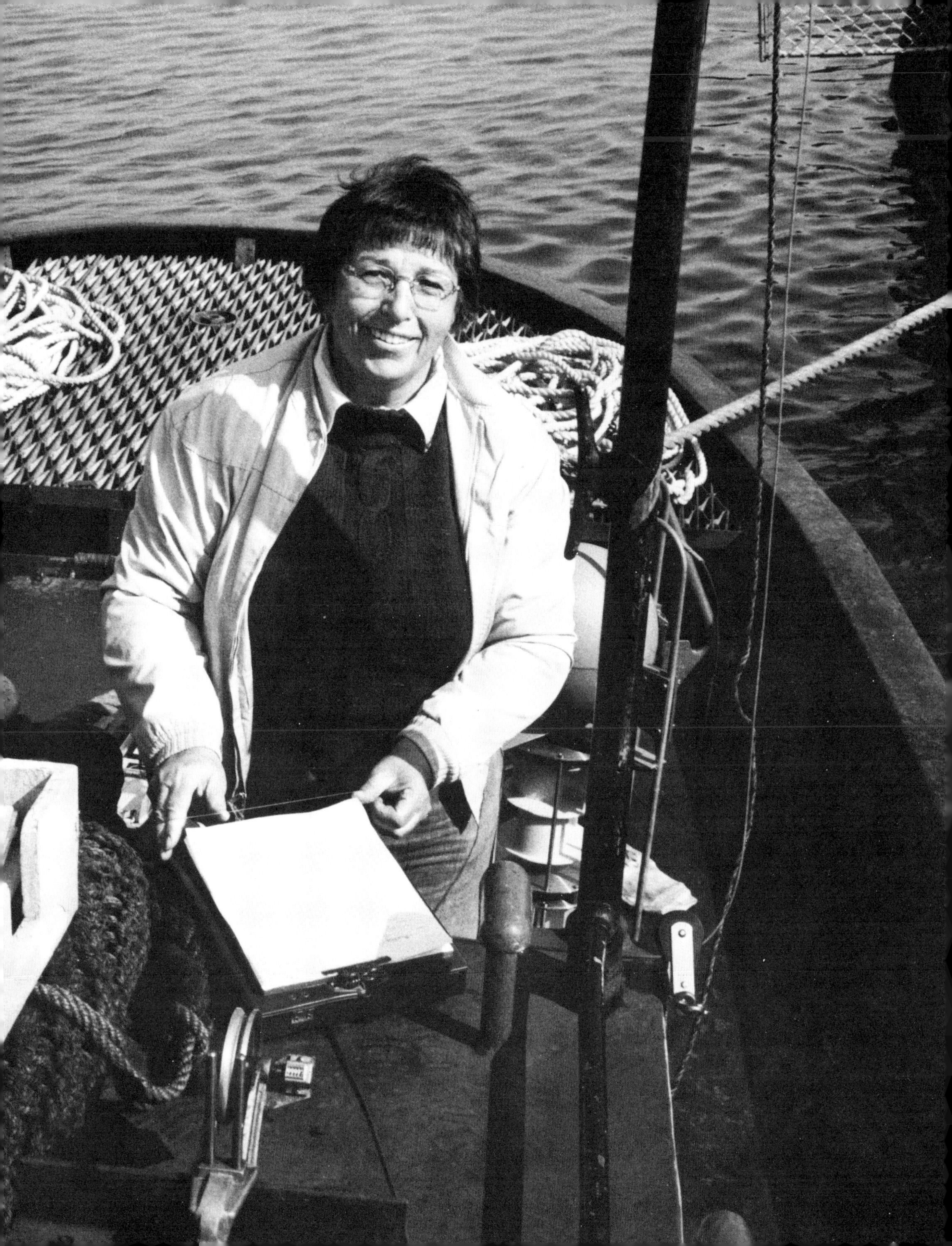

research. When I create my own projects, I can work on what interests me most, whether it is in Central or East Africa, India, Alaska or the continental United States.

Interest in travel and the outdoors helped me decide upon geology as a career. For a while I couldn't decide between biology and geology. I wanted to study the polar regions and it caused me to reason that there was earth everywhere, but there were not animals everywhere, so I chose geology. As I grew up, I learned that there are animals everywhere, too, even in the polar regions. I'm happy with my choice of geology, though, for I love the outdoors and enjoy doing something constructive that is of value to a community. I enjoy solving practical problems.

Some girls think that because geology involves field work, it is too dirty or rough for a girl, and that is definitely not so. When I am out on an oil rig, on a ship, or in a field camp, I find I am treated more courteously than I am in the city. When you have training to prepare yourself for your work and you know what you are doing, you get respect and cooperation from your co-workers. If you know your manners and concentrate on the business at hand, everyone wants to help.

As you might imagine, science and math are important to study if you are interested in a career in geology, but so is English. If you cannot properly communicate what you discover, the discovery is lost or muddled. There are many library books on the subject of geology, and you might like to look into some of the specialized fields: petroleum geology, ore geology, marine geology, engineering geology, ground water geology or environmental geology.

There is a great deal of confusion over the terms environmentalist and ecologist. An environmentalist needs knowledge of the environment, and that means geology or meteorology. An ecologist needs knowledge of living things and that means botany or zoology. The environmental experts and the ecology experts must work together. With cooperation, much can be done. For example, there is no need for droughts and floods in this day and age, nor for massive damage from earthquakes. If the talents of our scientists are properly used, and funds are raised for studies in these problems, they can be eliminated.

Such very basic problems of the environment and how people can live are what geology is all about. After all, everything that people have and make comes from the rocks and minerals contained in and on the earth.

Sandra Olsen PHYSICIAN

When I was growing up, a doctor lived across the street from us. I can remember watching him hurry out the door with his black bag to make house calls, and imagining him arriving in the nick of time to deliver a baby, fix a broken leg, or save a patient from death. As I grew older, I began to think that perhaps my image of a doctor's life was too dramatic and glamorous, and I put it out of my mind. I went to a liberal arts college, not sure of what I wanted to be.

Near graduation, the idea of studying medicine gradually worked its way back into my thoughts. Almost without realizing it, I was making up my mind to be a doctor. I took a summer job as a scrub technician—a rather routine and dirty-work job—in the surgical department of a local hospital. I picked up the towels, cleaned up operating areas, put things away and handed tools to the doctors. It seemed to be the best way for me to test my ambition. I figured that if I could stand the daily grind and the worst parts of the job, I would be sure I was not just following a childhood daydream but a childhood ambition.

The hardest part was getting into medical school. Even though my college grades were very good, at that time the medical schools made entrance difficult for girls. They felt that women would quit being doctors once they got married and had children. This would waste an expensive education. But many women have proved that this is not so, by combining family life and medicine so well that the medical schools have had to start changing their ways.

Once I was accepted into medical school, the prejudice I had felt about entrance was dropped and I was treated like everyone else. There were many years of study, but it was fascinating study. I remember my classmates teasing one another that they would get sick while witnessing their first operation. But most of us were so anxious to learn, that when the time came, we forgot about being sick.

After medical school I interned, that is, practiced being a doctor at a hospital where older doctors could help and advise. I

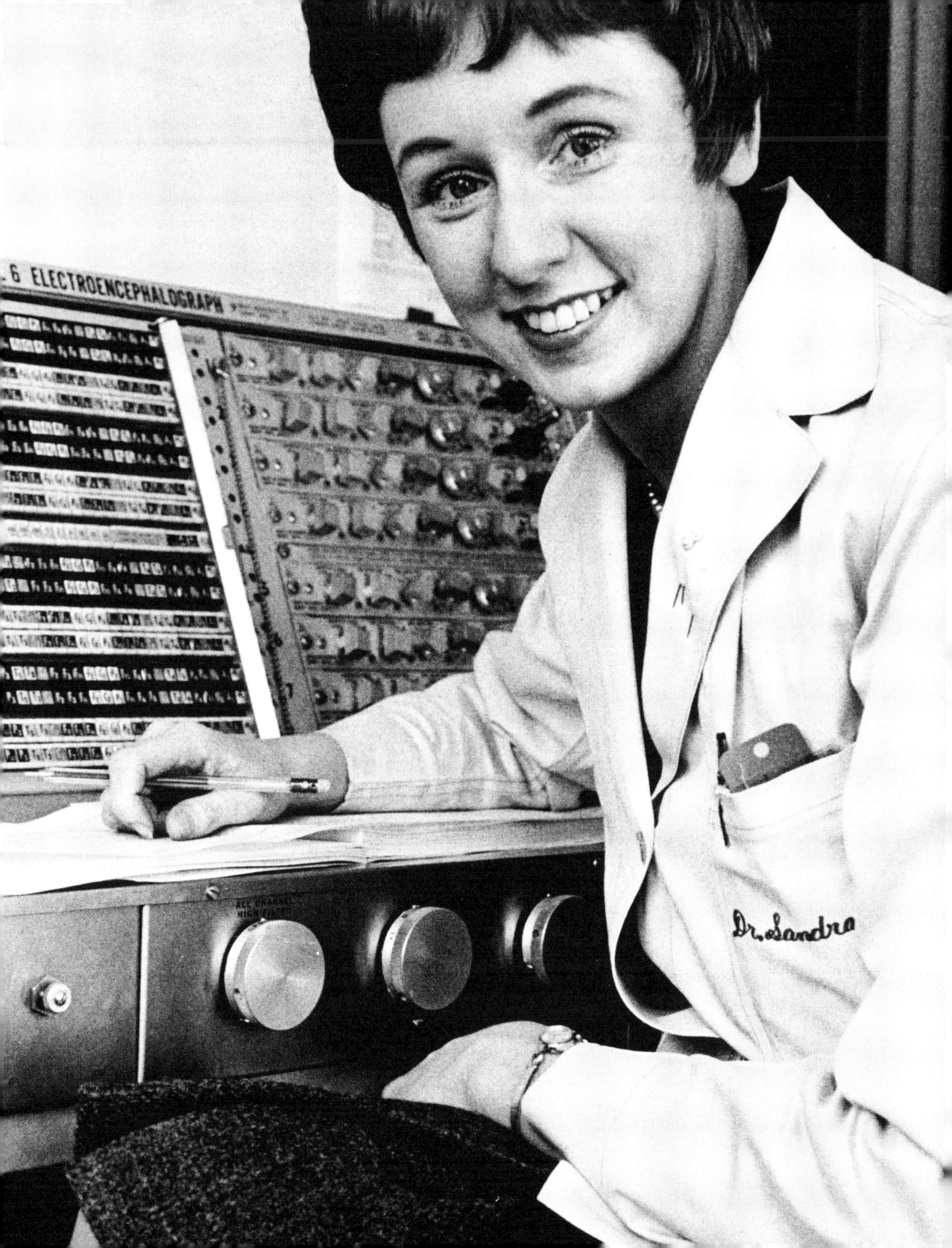
ELECTROENCEPHALOGRAPH
Dr. Sandra

assisted with operations, helped deliver babies, and began to feel very much a doctor.

The satisfaction I imagined as a child was just as I had imagined it. I love dealing with people and helping them control their problems. My specialty is neurology—the study of the nervous system. I treat people for epilepsy, concussions and other brain disorders. This is often done by electroencephalographs, that is, tests of brain waves. A child may be brought to my office who has been having frightening epileptic seizures. With the tests I do, I can decide what medication and treatment is needed to control the illness, and so give the child a normal life.

When girls ask me for advice about going into medicine, I tell them to pick whatever medical or surgical field attracts them most; you can't help doing well at what really interests you. Many women go into fields that have regular hours. This is a help to women like me who have small children. But the field of medicine is changing constantly and soon there may be regular hours in every area of medicine. When you've found the field that is for you, you've found a treasure. Stick to it and work!

Judy Joye OCEANOGRAPHER

My career in oceanography began with an interest in scuba diving, and that interest developed by pure chance. I was at a small party, and someone near me said, "When you wear a face mask, you can see as clearly underwater as you can on land." That amazed me, because then, in 1958, I had never heard of a face mask or of the other fascinating underwater sights and sensations this person described.

I decided that on my vacation, I would go to Mexico and try skin diving. I did, and was overwhelmed with what I had seen. Underwater, everything moves with a gentle swaying motion. It's like watching a gentle wind bend and sway a large field of wheat. The colors underwater are exotic—you never see a yellow unless it's the brightest yellow any artist could mix, and you never see a blue unless it's the brightest, most iridescent blue anyone has seen. Then, there's the sensation of weightlessness, which cannot be described. Organizations teach blind people to swim and scuba dive so they can experience this strange sensation. It's similar to the weightlessness that astronauts experience.

When I came back from my vacation, I immediately signed up for lessons at the YMCA so I could learn more about diving, and especially scuba diving. Scuba is the abbreviation for self-contained-underwater-breathing-apparatus, which means that you carry a tank of compressed air on your back and breathe through a regulator attached to the tank. This enables you to stay under water without surfacing to breathe.

After taking all of the YMCA's diving courses, I was asked to remain as an instructor. I knew of no professional women divers at the time, and I was the first woman to be graduated from this course. When a manufacturer of diving equipment would come to the "Y" looking for someone to demonstrate his equipment at a show, I often got the job *because* I was a woman, and they thought that a woman diver would make the demonstration more interesting. I got more and more photo assignments for commercials, and jobs for lectures and demonstrations of underwater equipment. So I decided to quit my job on a magazine and go into diving full time.

As a professional diver, it was *not* an advantage to be a

woman. I inspected such underwater things as boat hulls, piers and wrecks. The people who hired divers had never worked with a woman diver before and were afraid to hire me. So I put my name in the telephone directory as J. Joye, Diver. When clients would call, they would assume that when a woman's voice answered the phone that she must be the diver's wife or secretary. They would ask, "Is Mr. Joye there?" And I would answer, "No, but can *I* help you?" They would then tell me what they needed done, thinking I was taking the message for a male diver. But I fooled them and would show up in my diving gear to do the job. By the time the shock had worn off, I had finished the job, and done it well, so there was no way they could object. And of course, they had fooled themselves by assuming all divers were men.

Gradually I became interested in doing more serious work and began to study oceanography. A diver puts a tank on his or her back, goes underwater, takes pictures, spears fish, et cetera. But an oceanographer does more scientific work, more constructive work, and contributes something that furthers knowledge and develops new techniques for studying underwater life.

In the early 1960's there were few universities that taught oceanography, as it was a new science that was just developing. I did a tremendous amount of reading and eventually collected 500 technical books and thousands of reprints of articles. I read every new book I could find about oceanography as soon as it was published. In this way I grew with the science. Participating has been a wonderful mental challenge—like being in aviation during the days of the Wright brothers and open-cockpit airplanes. But I consider myself to be the last one to "sneak in through the plumbing" by diving and teaching myself. Now a girl must have a degree, and the more education she acquires in different fields, the better off she will be. Those fields of study that apply best to oceanography are biology, physics and engineering. There are many colleges where one can study and major in oceanography.

As an oceanographer, I go to many conferences, lecture, and write for technical journals. While I still do a lot of diving,

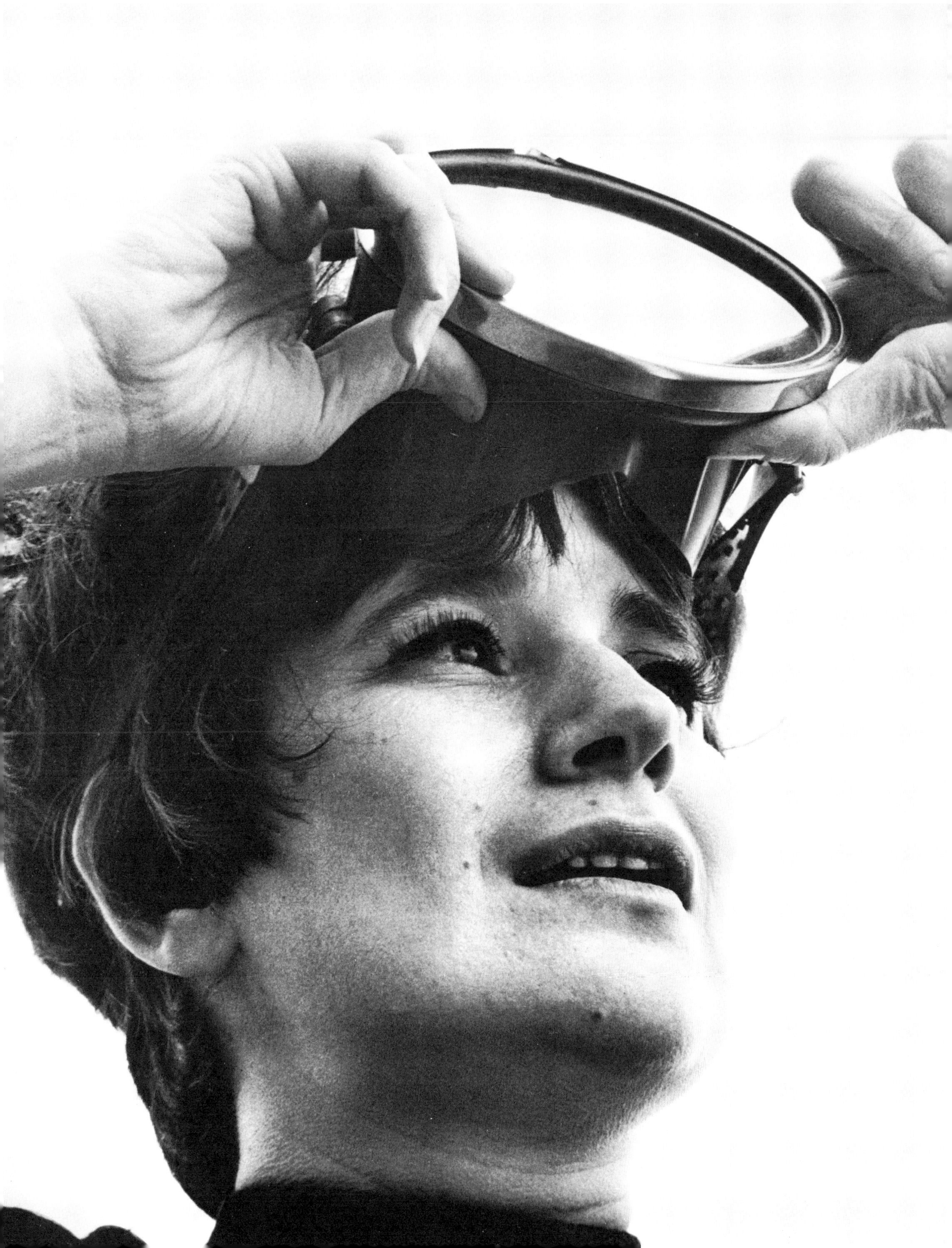

what I dive *for* has changed. For example, instead of untangling a line from a boat's propeller so that its owner can win a boat race, I collect samples of marine life for pharmaceutical companies that are trying to find cures for many diseases, incuding cancer. So far this has been my favorite project. Expeditions to collect marine specimens must be carefully organized, and a crackerjack knowledge of biology is essential. The possibility of developing a whole new family of antibiotics through this study of marine organisms is an exciting goal.

My safety rules for diving have never changed. I don't go in for heroics. I do not consider a person to be a good diver because she or he has dived deeper than the next diver or has had face-to-face combat with sharks. Taking unnecessary risks can not only get you hurt, it can ruin the job on which you are working. Part of a diver's training is the study of venomous fish and the behavior of marine animals. These creatures should be respected. It takes no training to go diving, but it takes a lot of training to *be* a diver. Many stores will not rent you diving equipment unless you have a certificate from an authorized school such as the YMCA.

When I dive in cold water, I wear a black wet suit for warmth. It's a tight rubber suit that covers me from head to toe. When the water is medium-warm, I wear a red dancer's leotard and tights. My reason for favoring red is that underwater, red is the first color to disappear from the spectrum as sunlight filters through the water. As a surface swimmer, a boat can see red for a long distance away, but to a fish or shark, red looks like black and blends with the scenery.

Some underwater animals are attracted by bright colors, such as white, orange or yellow. One of my funniest experiences involved a large, 100-pound turtle that was attracted to the bright wires attached to my underwater camera. He grabbed them in his mouth and began chewing. Well, I knew better than to try taking food from an animal's mouth, but this camera had cost nearly a thousand dollars! I couldn't let him eat it so I began pulling the wires from him. He got very angry and grabbed my foot in his mouth. It was quite a scuffle, and I had to put both hands around his throat and begin choking him before he would let go.

The most amazing thing about oceanography is that it is such a new science. Two-thirds of the earth's surface is covered by water and yet very little of the oceans and their mysteries has been explored and studied. The oceans are the last frontier left on earth. Right now nations are deliberating the question of who owns the resources in the seas. Each nation owns the resources for a few miles out from their coastlines, but right now, no one owns the resources beyond the limits of national jurisdiction. The United Nations is trying to solve this problem by stating that, "these resources are the common heritage of all mankind."

When I talk to teenagers about oceanography, I like to emphasize the fact that in so many fields a person may go into, he or she can adapt this work to the oceans. If you become an engineer, you can develop buoy systems, which are sophisticated electronic packages that make various measurements of ocean temperature and salinity. If you become a dietitian, you can create special diets and foods for astronauts and aquanauts. As an architect, you can design underwater habitats in which diver-scientists can live and study underwater life.

Two-thirds of the earth cannot be overlooked as it has been in the past. Who knows what new marvels will be developed from this last frontier? This is why I encourage people in all fields to adapt their work to some part of the oceans—I tell them to keep one foot dry and the other foot wet.

Mary Wahlman PHARMACIST

As a young child, I was never sick so I never had occasion to even see a pharmacist. I wouldn't have wanted to be one then because I thought they must be spooky characters, like magicians or alchemists, mixing up potions. Of course, I learned they were none of these.

Just in case you, too, have never been sick, I'll explain what a pharmacist does. When the doctor orders a particular medicine for you, of the kind you cannot just pick up from the shelves in a drugstore, you take the prescription to the pharmacist. The pharmacist picks out the right medicine from various pills, capsules, powders or liquids, marks it with the doctor's directions and other necessary information, and explains to you how to take it properly.

When a medicine doesn't require a prescription, I sometimes help people pick out what they need for what ails them. Because they help people find the right medicine for simple ailments, pharmacists are sometimes called the poor man's doctor. They sometimes help by telling a person *not* to buy a medicine off the shelves, when that person needs more than just a simple medicine and should see a doctor instead.

Work for a degree in pharmacy takes five years, and there's a lot to be learned. A pharmacist must know the characteristics of many drugs, the tests for purity and strength of them, their effects and possible dangerous side effects, and how to store each drug properly. Proper dosages for children and adults, and proper dosages for different uses of each drug must be learned. This is particularly important, because all drugs can be dangerous if wrongly used. Depending on the dosage, a drug may save a life or take a life. One of my professors in college used to impress this fact on us by reminding us that even water can be a poison when taken improperly. For example, in the case of a near-drowning, water left in the lungs can be toxic, and poison to the body.

New drugs are being discovered all the time, and we keep up on these new discoveries by reading special material that comes packaged with each new drug. Sometimes the drug salesperson explains the use of new products.

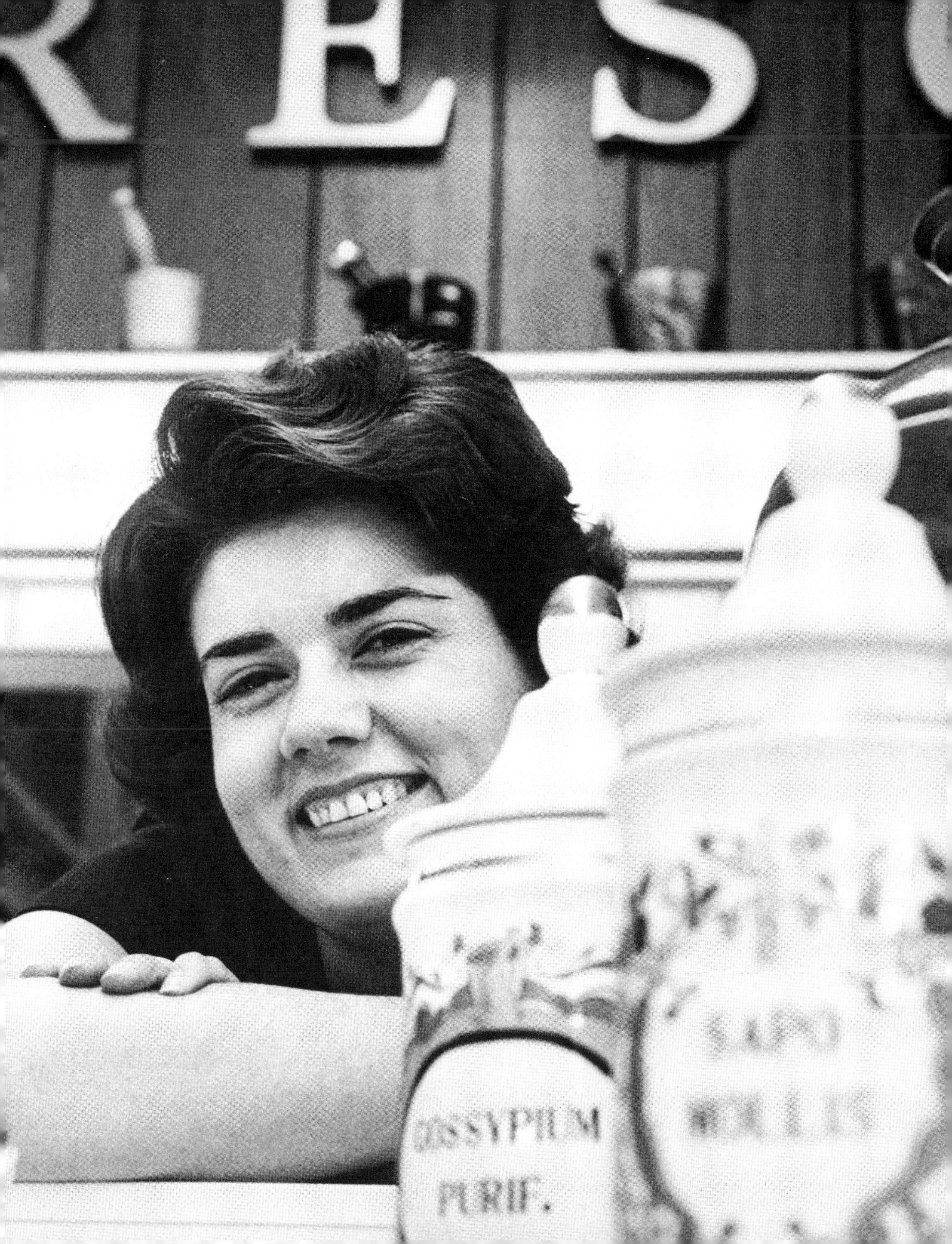
GOSSYPIUM
PURIF.
SAPO
MOLLIS

The doctor and pharmacist share the responsibility to see that a prescription is correct. If a busy doctor makes a mistake in dosage while writing a prescription, it's up to the pharmacist to catch that mistake. When a dosage seems way off, I inquire as to what the medication is being used for; if that does not explain it, I call the doctor who wrote it. Usually a doctor will correct a mistake immediately on the phone. Although this has never happened to me, if a doctor were wrong and would not correct the mistake, I could not go ahead and fill the prescription, saying that whatever happened would be the doctor's fault. I would have to refuse to fill it.

Laws change from time to time, and the government sends out information on what a pharmacist must do to comply with laws about drugs. Special forms must often be filled out for narcotic drugs.

A pharmacist may work in hospital pharmacies, community pharmacies, and for drug companies in research and sales work. Many pharmacists own their own drugstores.

I enjoy both hospital and community pharmacy work, though they are very different from one another. In hospitals you get into the field of clinical pharmacy, working along with the doctor to determine a drug regimen for a patient. Then you help to decide if the drugs used are working. You can help the physician in suggesting what to prescribe, and you can watch the patient's progress. In a community pharmacy, the doctor is in his or her office, too far away to confer on a prescription and too busy to ask your advice. You cannot check on the patient's progress to find out whether or not the drug is working. However, you can see the patient face to face when you fill the prescription, and make sure she or he understands how to take the medicine properly. In most community pharmacies, the pharmacist lives in that same community, and feels closer to the people she sees than she would in a hospital.

In some university hospitals, an ideal situation is being created by putting pharmacists at each nursing station so that they can see the patients they are dispensing medicine to, can make sure the patients understand the effects of the medicine and its proper use, and can check up on how effective the medicine is.

This kind of communication is very important. When people have bad reactions to drugs, they often call their pharmacists if they cannot reach their doctors. One pharmacist I know has a business in a Latin-American community and does not yet speak Spanish. He makes sure he hires helpers who do speak Spanish and who can translate peoples' questions to him and help him explain the medicines to them.

One question people jokingly ask me is if there's a special course in college to teach you how to read doctors' handwriting on prescriptions. There isn't such a course, naturally, but somehow, you can usually make out any handwriting once you get used to doing it.

There seem to be more and more women going into the field of pharmacy. When I graduated, my class was only ten per cent women, and the last class I heard of at my school was fifty per cent women.

I chose the field completely out of the blue, while reading the introduction in a chemistry textbook in high school. It mentioned that pharmacy was one of the fields that a study of chemistry could lead to. I liked chemistry, and decided to go on to college to study pharmacy. It only took me a minute to make my decision, and I didn't change it.

If you are interested in the field, you may be able to find books on the subject in the library, or better yet, take a chemistry course. And unless you are unusually healthy and never see a pharmacist, you might ask questions of your own pharmacist next time you visit the drugstore to have a prescription filled.

Clara Vanderbilt PHYSICIAN'S ASSOCIATE

The idea of physicians' associates is a new concept completely. A physician's associate, or PA, receives training similar to that of a doctor, but not for as long a time. It's a very practical course of training and prepares the PA to work along with a physician, doing many jobs previously done by the doctor alone.

The field is much different from nursing. While a nurse cares for an ill person, the doctor treats the illness. A nurse follows treatment and medicine orders of the doctor and makes the patient comfortable; the doctor decides what is wrong and makes him well. A PA can fit both these roles to some extent. She can take on some of the doctor's tasks in treating the illness but has more time for the little things a nurse might do to help the patient's morale. Have you ever heard of a practical nurse? Well, a PA might be called a practical doctor. I like my son's explanation: "Mommy does things like doctors do, but she's not called doctor, she's called Mrs. Vanderbilt."

The new concept of physicians' associates can help to solve some of the most pressing medical care problems in our country. Phyicians' associates can help in areas where there are drastic doctor shortages, like the city ghettos and the Appalachians.

For example, in the Appalachians there are places where the people are spread out over large areas in rough, mountainous country. It's hard for them to get to the few doctors who practice there. A doctor with two associates could see as many patients as three doctors, by establishing an office in some central area and sending the associates to the outlying districts. The associate could take care of everyday problems like colds, stitches and checkups, but could send more serious cases to the doctor.

In a ghetto area, PA's work along with doctors in clinics. The PA can examine a patient, take a history of the illness, order tests and report the findings to the doctor. The doctor will then make a diagnosis and prescribe for the patient.

Private physicians and surgeons also employ physicians' associates, and in some areas they are used for rescue work. In California, I've heard there are helicopter rescue programs that employ former army medics.

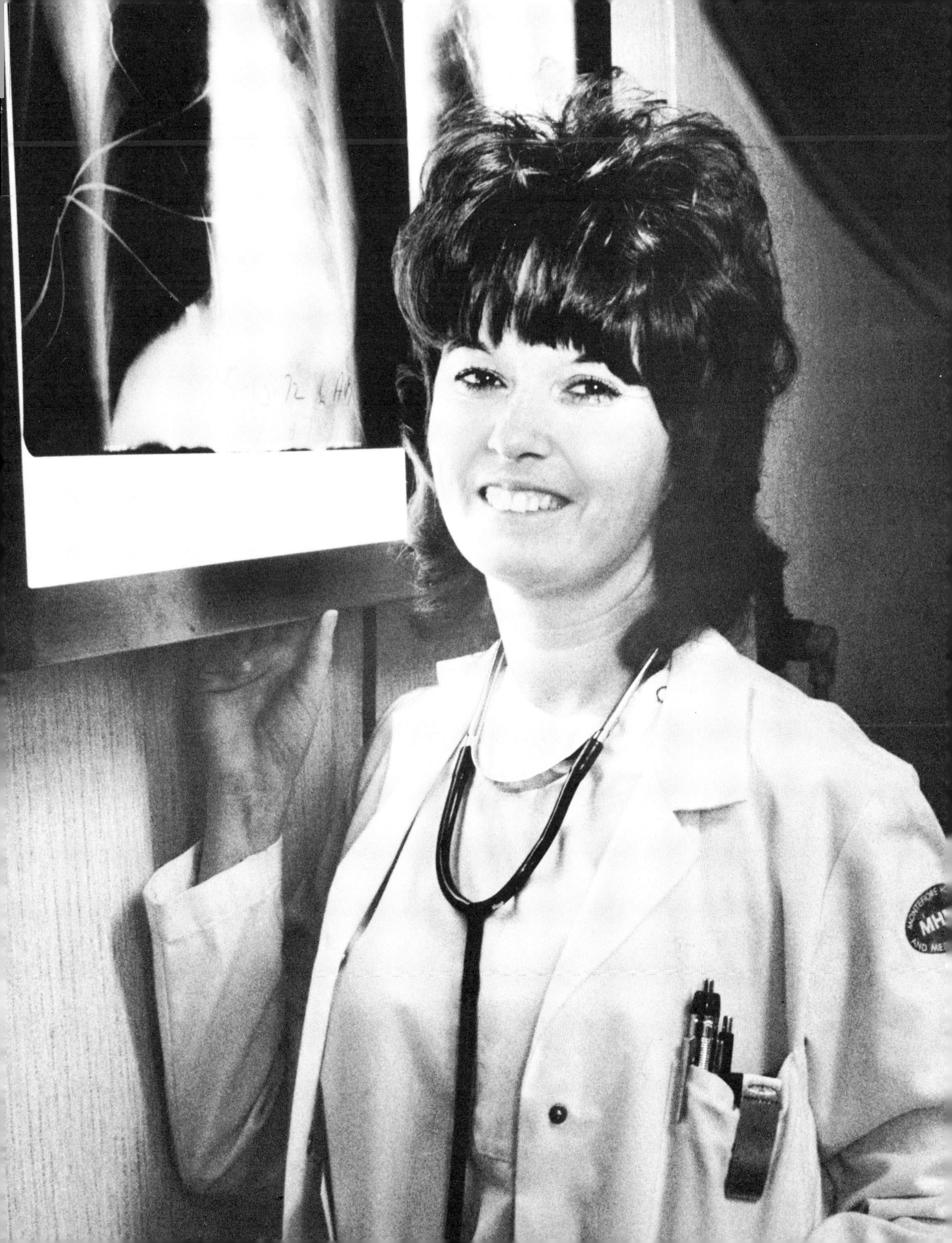

A PA is not self-employed like a doctor, but is hired by a private doctor, clinic or hospital. Naturally a PA does not make as much money as a doctor, but the training is not as long and the responsibilities are not as great. However, it's a continuous learning situation, and you can go as far as you want after completing school. It is a wonderful field for a girl who is interested in medical work, especially if she is more interested in the diagnosis and treatment of the patient rather than the nursing care, or if she cannot afford the long training required of a doctor. This was the case for me.

When I was a child I was always picking up wounded birds from the road, trying to save them with little splints made of sticks and food from medicine droppers. I thought I'd be a nurse when I grew up. But I got married at 16, went to work soon after, and had three children early in my marriage. I couldn't afford nursing school at that time; I had to work. But I did the next best thing and worked at various jobs in different hospitals, learning as much as I could at each job. I did office work, laboratory work, and had jobs in which I did many nursing tasks, because of the shortage of nurses at that time. All the while I asked questions about everything. There was a wonderful doctor at one hospital who would give me an entire lecture in answer to each question I asked. A university medical school was associated with this hospital and the students made rounds with the doctors visiting patients as part of their training. I went along on these and learned all I could. Soon I was more interested in medical diagnoses and treatment than in nursing care.

Throughout this time, I worked at catching up on the education I had cut short when I quit high school. I took a high school equivalency test and then signed up for evening classes in English and science.

One day I heard of the new Physicians' Associates Program that had been started by a doctor teaching at Duke University. It had been originally set up to give added training to those young men who had been trained as medics in Vietnam. The idea was that with the shortage of doctors in the U.S., it was a shame to waste the training these men had had. But the program was also open to anyone who had experience in the health field, a high school diploma, chemistry and biology courses and some college work. This program was exactly what I had been looking for. I applied as soon as possible, and was admitted.

The training was similar to that of the medical students who were studying to be doctors. In fact, we had many of our courses together. Ours was a two-year course, however. The first ten months we studied anatomy, clinical medicine and physical diagnosis. We also had laboratory courses, chemistry and microbiology. The last fourteen months we worked with patients in hospital wards, making rounds with the doctors and listening to lectures. We did histories and physicals of patients and presented this information to the doctors along with our opinions of what was wrong with each patient and why we thought so. We learned by supervised practice.

I chose surgery as my special field, and on graduation was offered a job with a New York hospital as a surgical associate. It's an exciting place to be, for difficult cases from all over New York City are sent there.

There are both advantages and disadvantages in being a PA. On the minus side, patients who have never met a physician's associate are not sure of what to expect and may treat me as less than professional until they get to know me and understand how I fit into the health care team. On the plus side, I find that patients ask me questions they are afraid to ask their doctors. They sometimes feel that their questions may be stupid or silly and yet they want an answer very badly. It works the same way for me. Where a new young doctor might be afraid to admit he does not know something he feels he should, I can ask the doctors anything I need to know without a blow to my ego.

As the first woman on the surgery staff of my hospital, the only disadvantage I've had is that my hands are too small for even the smallest surgical gloves and I find myself having trouble with gloves that are too large—it's hard to keep from sewing the fingertips together as I take stitches for a patient. The hospital is solving this problem for me by having casts made of my hands, and gloves made to order from the casts.

The satisfactions of my work are truly great. It's good to know that my family is proud of me and my children are interested in my work. My daughter likes to play at doctoring her doll and her cat, just as I enjoyed caring for sick birds. When her cat had kittens, she told me she delivered them.

My son was fascinated by the bandages we use to make casts. He wanted to use them to dress up as an accident victim for Halloween, so I got some for him, and showed him how they worked. He gave himself a bandaged head, casts on both feet, and a cast and sling on one arm. He really was a sight.

The greatest satisfaction comes from the work itself. I would be wrong if I said that I spend 90 hours a week in the hospital because I'm so concerned with the health of mankind—I do it because of the personal gratification I get from it. If a patient comes in and says, "I'm hurting, help me," and if I can find out what's wrong and help, it's good to know that the patient feels better. But it makes me feel good, too, knowing that it was something I'd studied and learned that enabled me to make this patient feel better. When a patient refuses to go to the operating room until he is sure I will be there, I feel great to know I've inspired so much confidence in someone—even if it's three o'clock in the morning when the patient insists I come. For life to be meaningful, we all need something that will give us this sense of gratification, of self-esteem.

Bonnie Sedlak DEVELOPMENTAL BIOLOGIST

In developmental biology, one studies the development of a caterpillar into butterfly, egg into chick, and so forth. I study the development of just one tiny cell at a time. By watching the changes in that one small cell from day to day, I can gain many valuable facts about the whole insect or animal.

The technique I use most often in these studies is electron microscopy. While a regular microscope magnifies 100 times, an electron microscope magnifies from 10,000 times and up. In using it I look at cells which I measure in angstroms. An angstrom unit is a ten-millionth of a millimeter and a millimeter is smaller than a tenth of an inch. Imagine dividing an inch into ten parts—then take one-thousandth of that and that's still 10,000 times too big, compared to what I'm working with. So you can imagine how small the cells are that I view through this microscope. To cut a section of a cell for viewing, we use a tiny diamond-edged knife and use a microscope while cutting.

In studying the heart of a fly, for example, I look at one small cell. If the whole heart were magnified as large as that small part, the picture would fill two rooms. And yet that small part can tell me important things about the whole heart.

I'll demonstrate this by telling you about a project a friend of mine is working on. The Muscular Dystrophy Foundation is supporting his study in hope that it will help explain the disease of muscular dystrophy—a disease which deteriorates the muscles. My friend is studying cells from rats' brains. He looks at the junction, or crossroad, in them between a nerve cell and a muscle to see how a nerve tells a muscle what to do. Once he finds out how this happens he will be one step closer to finding out why this sometimes does not happen. He may find an application to muscular dystrophy.

By studying cells as they develop day after day, one can see how a cell should look when it is developing properly. Therefore, it will become possible to see when a cell is not developing properly. If the biologist can tell what the differences are between a properly and non-properly developing cell, he or she can help medicine discover what is missing and what can be added to aid proper function.

A girl who is interested in being a biologist should naturally study chemistry, biology and math in high school, but she should also take as many liberal arts courses as she can. To think creatively in any field, it's necessary to be well-rounded. She might also search for library books in other areas of biology, such as ion transport, fluid transport, biochemistry and biophysics. If her school encourages science projects, she should do as many as she can.

Research biologists are employed by universities, hospitals and industry. The same places employ research technicians who do not need a degree.

When I first began my study of biology in college, one of my main professors often tried to discourage me. If I didn't do well on a test, he would say, "Oh well, it doesn't matter, you'll get married soon and then you won't care about biology anymore." I knew that I would care about biology whether I was married or not and didn't let him discourage me. Later, when I had finished my undergraduate degree, he was the one to give me advice on where to get the best training in my field while studying for a master's degree. And when I had that degree and began looking for a job, I wrote to him, among others, for a job in the field of electron microscopy. Guess who was the one to come up with a job for me? That very prof who had tried to discourage me in the beginning!

I work now in the electron microscopy lab of a university, where I also teach. Although it takes great patience, I find laboratory work very satisfying, especially when I discover something new. It's necessary to check in the library at such times to make sure that my discovery hasn't already been made, for it would be silly to duplicate someone else's work. If I find that my discovery is new, I publish a paper (an article in a scientific magazine).

An example of this kind of discovery is something I began to study while still a student. In developing systems, biologists have always said that a cell must be juvenile to divide, and that

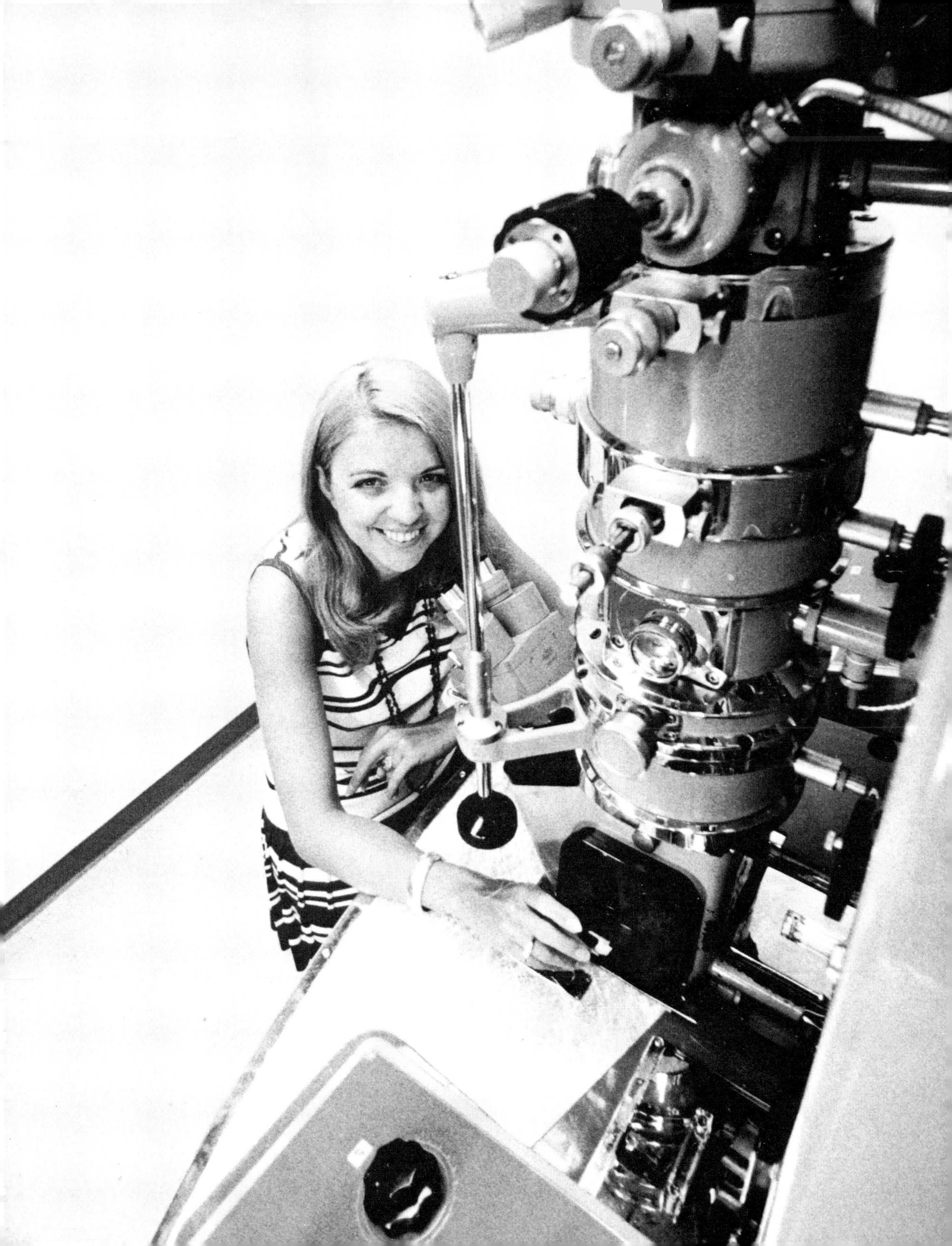

when a cell was fully developed, or mature, it would not divide. But I found in my system a cell that took on adult characteristics and *then* divided, going against all biological laws, which made it very interesting. Using an electron microscope gives one living proof of a discovery. Although another science might show that a process may exist, I can take pictures through the microscope day after day of that process actually happening.

I find it exciting to think that what I'm looking at has never been seen before, and that if I look at it carefully enough and relate it to what other scientists have done before, I might be saying something that's very important and very far-reaching—all with one tiny cell.

Aida Khalafalla BIOPHYSICIST

In one of my classes at the university we studied the electrical properties of body tissues and I learned that our bodies act like resistors and electrical networks. We are like walking radios. I thought about this, and wondered why we couldn't apply this by trying to use these electrical properties to study human functions. We could help these radio-like aspects of the body to send messages to us.

Later on in my work, I was able to test my idea by using electronics to study these electrical properties of body tissues. A biophysicist uses the tools of physics to study the human body. I devised a machine, called the impedance plethysmograph, to do this. It uses a small and harmless electric current which is introduced into the body at the area that is to be tested. The amount of resistance to the current is measured. If the amount is not the normal amount, we know that the part of the body being tested is diseased.

When the machine is perfected and ready to be produced for hospitals, it can be used to do many medical tests painlessly and more accurately than they are now done. I have already used it to test for heart and lung diseases. Without touching the heart, it can measure the amount of blood being pumped out of a heart with each beat.

One of the uses I am most happy about is a test it can perform for unborn babies. When a woman is ill and must take medications late in a pregnancy, there is danger to the baby. Tests must be done to make sure that the baby is all right. Previously the only way to do these tests was very painful for the mother and dangerous to the unborn baby. But with this new machine, the tests can be done safely and painlessly.

In my present job as a research scientist for a company, I am free to come up with my own ideas, as long as they have practical applications, and present them at meetings. The company raises money for the research and I then invent ways to turn my ideas into useful techniques and machines, such as the one I described. In any major project, scientists must depend upon one another and cooperate in sharing their research or there can be no progress. This is why scientists must go to many conferences.

The traveling to conferences and meeting other scientists is a part of my work that I love. I have always wanted to travel, and I find that I really enjoy working with scientists.

I might not have gone into the field, however, if it hadn't been for a helpful teacher. When I was thirteen I took a science course and found that everything about it interested me. I would come home from school excited about what I had learned and insist that my father listen while I explained to him how fascinating atoms were. He must have been very bored, but he wanted to encourage me and would often listen for hours. He nicknamed me "Doctor Aida."

My teachers encouraged me too, and I began to be especially interested in physics. But when it came time for college, I was afraid that physics might be too hard, that perhaps it was a "man's job" and that I was starting college young and should take something easier. I applied to study French, thinking I would at least get to travel and perhaps work at the United Nations.

My high school teacher, who was a friend of my father, called him one day and asked how my plans were coming for studying science in college. Father replied that I was taking French literature instead. My teacher almost collapsed. He said, "She is not! She is a scientist! I am going to do something about this!" The next day, he came over to our house and went with us to the college where he helped me change my major to science. I'm very glad he did, for I was wrong in my fears that physics would be hard for me. If you really like a subject it is always easy. For people like me, it is sometimes easier to talk in equations than words, when describing scientific problems.

And my dreams of travel were fulfilled in the bargain. I recently went to Brussels and soon will go to Russia for scientific conferences. And I recently went with my husband to Japan where he attended a conference.

My husband is a physical chemist. It helps that he is also a scientist, for we can understand one another's work. Our sons are interested in our work too, especially the oldest, who loves math

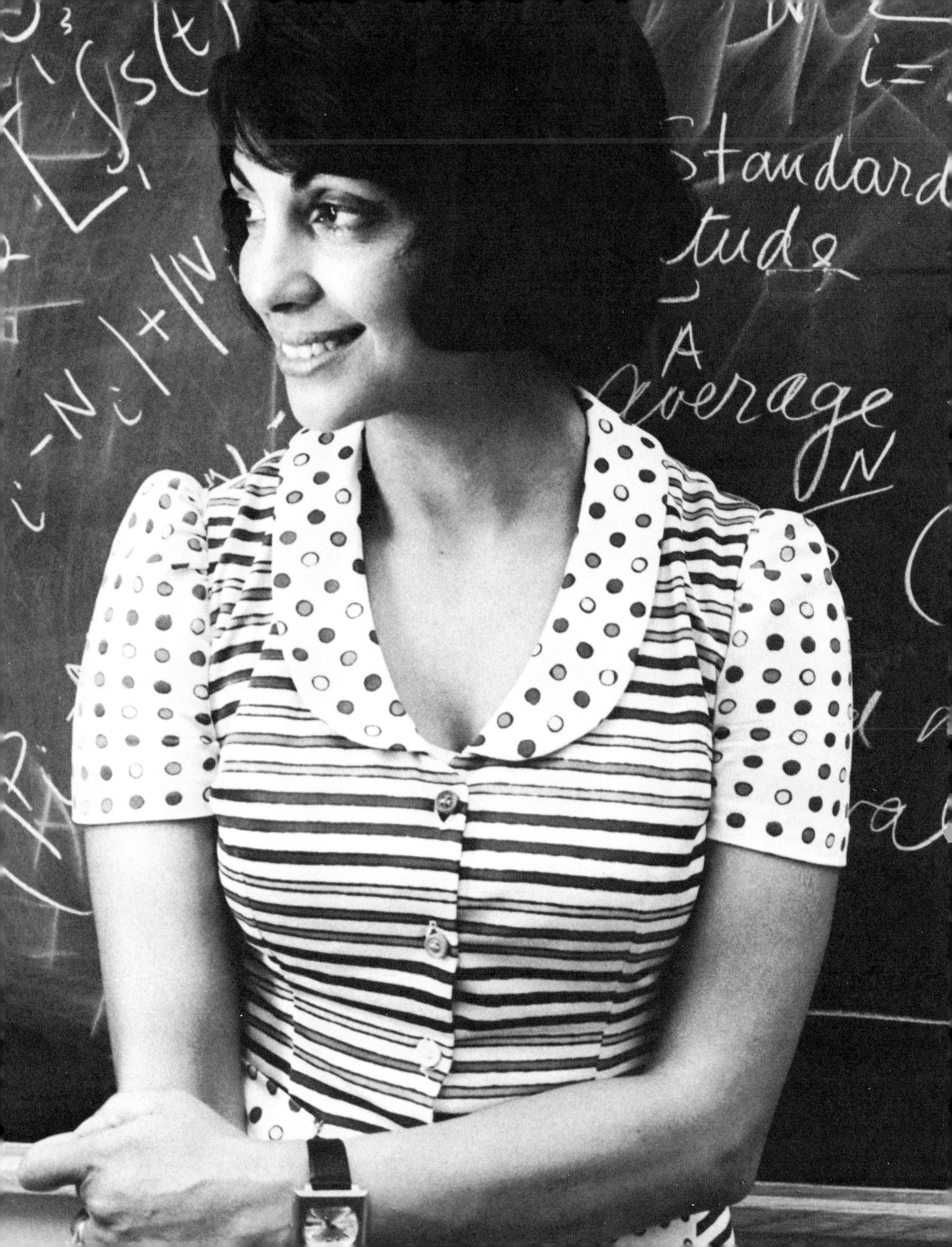

Standard
A
average

and is scientifically oriented. He recently presented me with a collage he had made. He had saved all the newspaper articles that had appeared about my work and made them into a collage, carefully decorated with colored paper.

When I was first married and we returned from our honeymoon, I cooked something my aunt had taught me for our first meal. My husband ate it and smiled, but I could see he was not happy. He said, "Why don't I take a turn at cooking tomorrow?" I was delighted to find out the next day that he was a gourmet cook—so much better at it than I that I have let him do the cooking ever since. He goes about it in the same way he goes about his work as a chemist, in a very orderly way. And he says that cooking is much like chemistry.

For a girl who is interested in physics or research science, I would say she should do well at school of course, but also read all the extra books she can get on her subject. This is true of any subject. Many universities and reasearch centers have open-house days. You might call and find when these are, and visit their labs. If you or your family knows someone with a job in such a place, ask them if you can visit; it's what I did as a girl. And don't be afraid to change when a new field interests you more than your old one. I got my B.S. degree in physics and chemistry when I was living in Egypt; I went to England to study medical physics and then to the University of Minnesota for my Ph.D. degree in biophysics.

Many girls think that the very smartest people are the only ones who can study science, but this is not at all true. A person who is good at science is simply good at science, just as another may be good at history. Neither is smarter than the other.

It is important that there be both men and women in the research sciences, for women have different experiences than men, and this causes them to notice some things a man might not notice—and vice versa.

I get the most satisfaction in my work from new ideas and inventions—from doing something that has not been done before. It feels very good to get up at a scientific conference and explain something useful that I have discovered.

TRADES, SERVICES & BUSINESSES

Linda McLennon   LETTER CARRIER

I love to be outdoors more than anything, and I've found a job that keeps me there. Of course letter carriers have to be out in snow, rain, heat or gloom of night, as the saying goes. The "gloom of night" is more like the crack of dawn and the snow may be three feet deep, but even so, I'm happy to be outdoors.

The idea of applying for this job came to me one day as I went out to get the mail (pretty easy to figure out; I don't know why I didn't think of it sooner) and I called the post office that day.

To be a post office employee, I had to take a civil service exam. Since the federal government is in charge of the postal service, our "boss" is the head of the post office department in Washington, D. C. The local postmaster is in charge of the local post office, so when I passed the exam I applied to him for a job. A letter carrier's job was open and I got it.

Then I learned to sort mail, cancel mail, memorize postage rates, learn all the mail routes and stay clear of dogs.

I've seen many cartoons of dogs chasing letter carriers, and they do seem to prefer us for chasing. I think perhaps that once they meet just one carrier who is afraid, they recognize the uniform and chase anyone in a letter carrier's uniform. Dogs sense fear and like to feel they are protecting their owner's property. Luckily for me, I'm not afraid of dogs, but if they chase me anyway, I can use a spray can that the post office supplies. It contains a chemical that dogs hate and run from, but that will not injure them.

Besides being out of doors, I enjoy walking, which of course I do a lot of. And the mail trucks we use in rural routes are fun to drive. The steering wheels are on the right, so that we can reach mailboxes alongside the road without getting out of the truck. Since American cars and trucks all have the steering wheel on the left, it takes a little getting used to.

Although I'm outdoors, I meet many people every day; they come to the door for their mail when they see me coming. After a few months on the route, I know most of the people, and those who are housebound really look forward to receiving their mail. It's the high point of their day. Stopping at so many homes, you

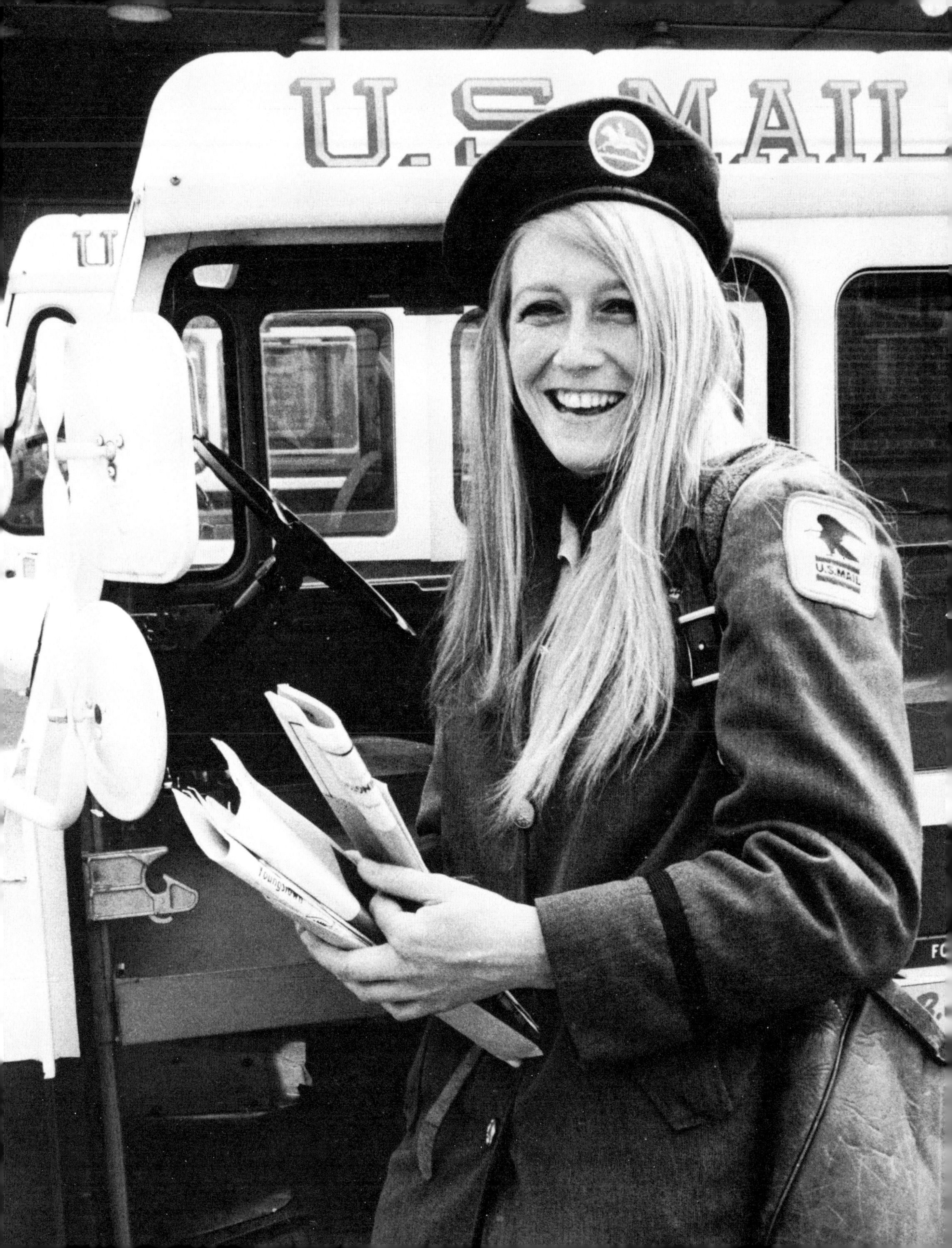
U.S. MAIL
U.S.MAIL

sometimes come at a lucky moment for the occupant. One letter carrier I know was stopping at a house just as a mother was calling for help. Her child was choking on something he had swallowed and she didn't know what to do. The letter carrier knew what to do, because the same thing had once happened to his own kid, and he helped save the child.

When I first started as a letter carrier, there were no other women carriers in my town. One morning I was given a special delivery letter to deliver at seven in the morning. The man who answered the door was angry at being awakened, and began yelling at his "mailman" as he opened the door. When he saw me, he was so surprised he stopped in the middle of a word.

If you're interested in being a letter carrier there's one very easy way to get your questions answered. Wait by your mailbox and a letter carrier is sure to come along about the same time each day, even during snow, rain or gloom of night.

Charlene Falkenberg   PILOT

Flying has fascinated me since I was young. I thought it must be wonderful to pilot a plane, but I didn't realize that I could be a pilot myself. I applied to be a stewardess, but at that time the airlines wouldn't take anyone over five-foot-seven, and I am tall. One day my husband suggested I take a few flying lessons. He had a private plane and thought it would be great if I knew how to handle it when we took trips together. Well, I took more than a few lessons; I got a license of my own. Then I went on to get a commercial license, which meant I could fly for hire (company planes, cargo, passenger airlines). Most of my time is spent teaching at a local airport school and flying my own plane. I'm glad my husband talked me into starting lessons.

Learning to fly was such an exciting, thrilling experience, that fear never entered my head. I just plain enjoyed flying too much. I never got airsick either, probably because I was having fun, was busy and had no time to think of it. I once got seasick in a very small boat on a very small lake, but don't get airsick even when I'm flying upside down or doing aerial stunts. I learned to unplug my ears in the plane by holding my nose, closing my mouth and trying to blow. Yawning and swallowing help too. I also discovered that I could dress as I did for driving a car—skirts and medium heels. The only thing I needed overalls for was overhauling my plane, when I get good and dirty.

I have few tales of danger to tell because I never fly in bad weather. That's not only foolishness and false bravery, but also unfair to other people in the plane and beneath you. However, I once ran into heavy clear-air turbulence (bumpy air you can't see coming) and the plane was pumped up and down 100 feet at a time. That was quite an experience. Most of the time I feel safer in the plane than in my car. There are fewer drivers to bump into and you can control the plane in many directions at once. I feel free and relaxed when flying and love the feeling of being part of the sky and the clouds. At the same time I love being in control of the plane and knowing just what I'm doing every minute.

As well as lessons in the air with a pilot and practice at flying solo, a pilot must have hours of class time on the ground. Ground

School is what I teach and it includes navigation, radio, meteorology (weather), weight and balance, airplane mechanics, instruments and computer. You can't fly safely without these ground courses. We use books, charts and the plane itself as study aids. It takes about a year to learn enough for a private pilot's license, and a commercial pilot's license takes longer.

There are schools at many private airports. You must be sixteen to fly solo and seventeen to receive a private pilot's license, but you can begin lessons and ground school as soon as you can understand them. I've known children who started as early as ten years old. If you've never been up in a small plane and would like to see what it's like, many small airports have Sunday rides for children for a few dollars. There are books on flying and on famous pilots that your local library may have, like *Night Flight* by Antoine de Saint-Exupery.

Besides jobs as pilots of company planes, private planes, cargo planes and airliners, there are jobs as meterologists, control tower operators, and many others. Although airlines didn't hire women as pilots in the past, they are doing so now.

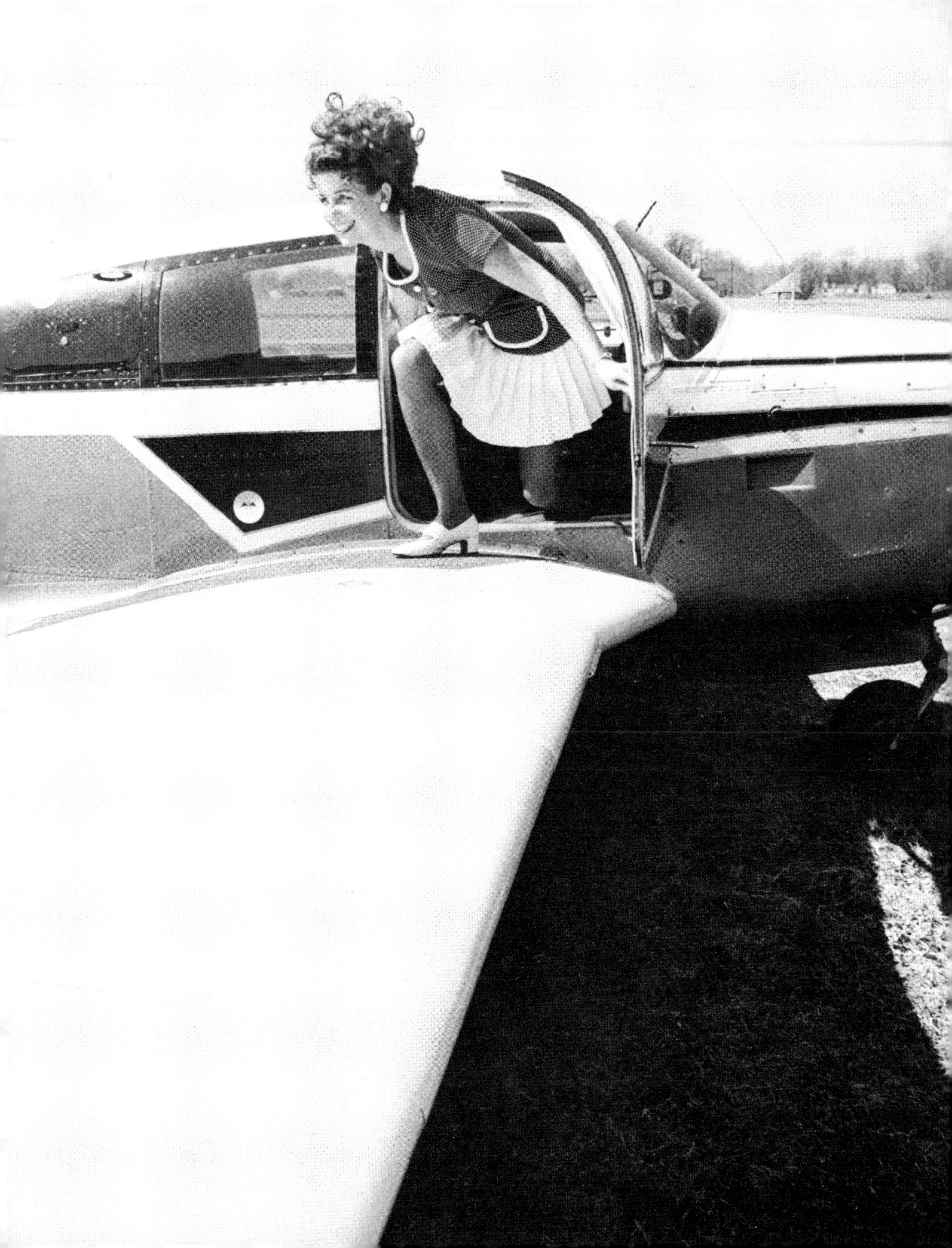

Marilyn Beis CARPENTER

Whenever we took aptitude tests in school, I scored high in mechanical ability. I knew I liked to work with my hands, but it wasn't until I was grown and already had another career and a family that it occurred to me I'd make a good carpenter. What did it was wanting to build a house—all by myself.

I heard stories of people going back to the land, building their own houses and living like pioneers. That movement is partly an interest in ecology, partly a desire to get away from it all. But what interested me most was the self-sufficiency of building your own home from scratch.

I knew I was good with my hands, but I didn't know how to build a house or even how to use all the tools needed to do it. If I was to build a house, I wanted to do it properly. And to do that I should be a carpenter. So I thought, well, I like it, it pays well, why not try it as a career.

To be employed by a builder, one must be a union carpenter, so I applied for the union apprenticeship program. A union is an association that sets standards for a trade and represents the people that belong to that trade. Apprenticeship is different from most schooling although it involves going to school. An apprenticeship program is set up by those who will employ you and the union you will belong to. They provide your training and agree to find you work. In return you agree to take a job when they find one for you, and while you are still in training, to work for less. For the carpenters' union, the apprentice program is set up by the union with support from the contractors (builders). Programs vary somewhat from state to state.

When I applied for the program, I took aptitude tests which determined that I was suited to carpentry. I signed a contract saying that I would work when work was available and the union signed a contract saying that they would find me work. Then I began classes.

The first twelve weeks are full-time school with classes in shop, general theory and drawing. In shop, we learned to use tools and work with wood. In general theory classes we studied math and related subjects; most of the math was elementary. In drawing

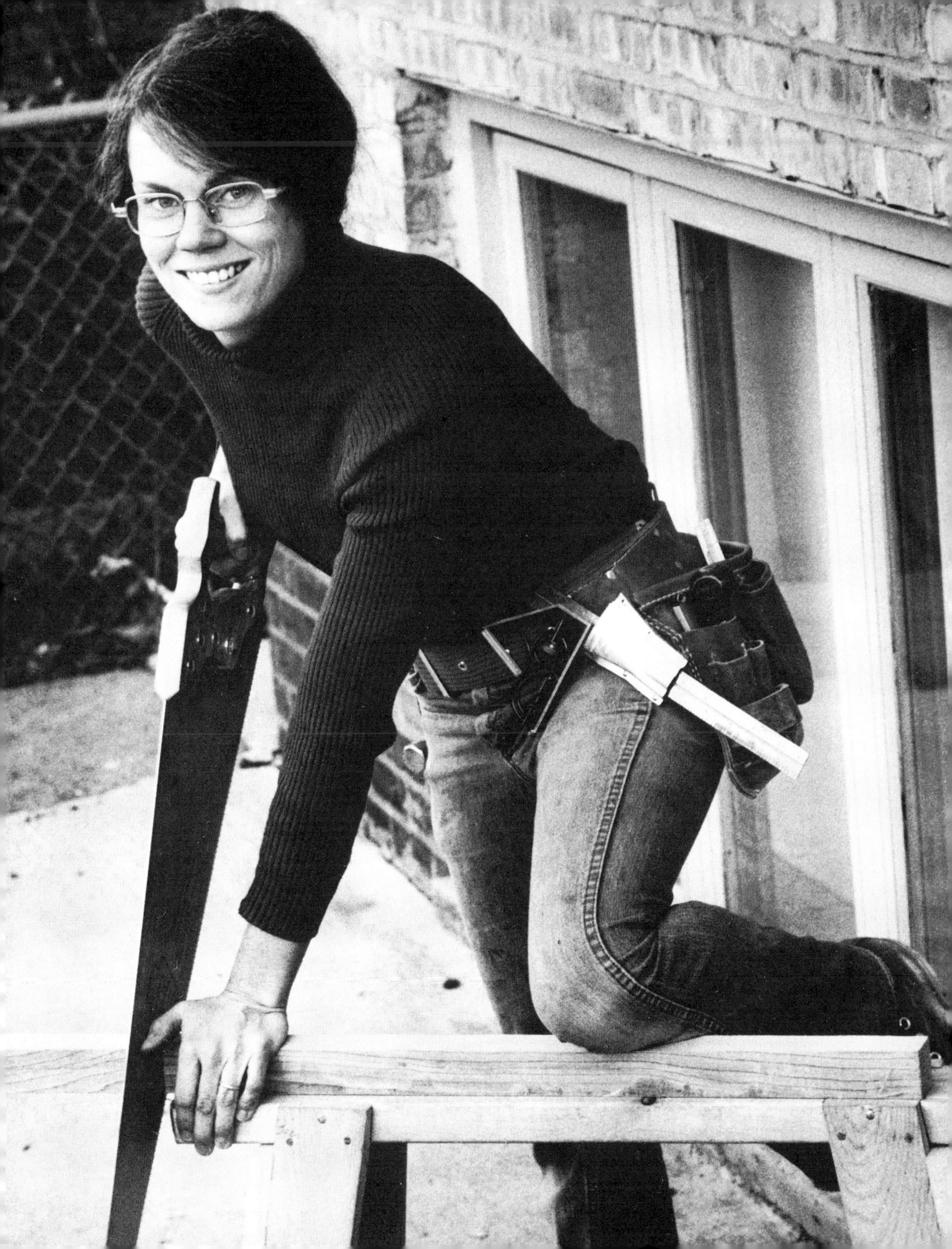

we learned mechanical drawing techniques and the reading of blueprints. A carpenter must know how to read blueprints in order to interpret the symbols that architects use.

After the first twelve weeks you are indentured, that is, you begin to work according to the agreement you signed when you began. For the first eighteen months you work four days a week and go to school one day. The union pays you for the day you are in school and the employer pays you for the four days that you work. For this first year you make 55% of what you will make when you are a fully trained carpenter. The second year you make 65%, the third 75%, and the fourth 90%. At the end of the four years you take another test, and on passing, you graduate from apprentice carpenter to journeyman carpenter.

Carpenters are the tradespeople most employed by construction companies, in terms of numbers and time with the project. The carpenter is the first person on the job—to lay out the building. This is done by laying out lines, and what are called batter-boards. The lines are stretched between the boards. This is called shooting the grades. Lines are laid according to the architect's plans, and they determine where the house is going to sit on the lot, what direction it is going to face, and how deep the foundation will be. Once the hole is dug, the carpenter must build forms for concrete to be poured into, and watch while it is being poured in case the forms break or bulge. Then of course, if the framework or skeleton of a house is wood, the carpenters build it. Everywhere there is wood involved—in sidings, roofing, drywalls and flooring—there must be carpenters to do it.

Carpenters also work on smaller jobs in homes and offices, making such things as built-in shelves and cupboards. This can be done on a free-lance basis, working for yourself.

My first regular job was with a construction company, working on a fine arts building for a university. The first day, I was looking at my hands for a moment and a fellow came up to me and said, "Oh, you're inspecting the new calluses on your hands." I answered that I had got my calluses doing housework, so I had had them for some time. Generally, there is no more heavy work in carpentry than in a home. The average woman who carries a twenty-pound child, groceries or laundry is capable of carrying anything one would need in carpentry.

As a woman in this field, the only real difference I have felt was the fact that I did not have a background of high school shop courses when I entered apprentice training. When I went to high school girls were not encouraged to take shop. In my case, I felt sure I could catch up, and I did, but it would have been nice to have had shop in high school. I would advise a girl with mechanical abilities to take whatever shop courses are offered.

My children are fascinated by the tools I work with, but they are too young to be allowed to play with them. I'll enjoy teaching them to use tools when they are older if they are interested. My son is especially enthusiastic about my job and wants to be both a lawyer like his father and a carpenter like his mother.

The most satisfying thing about my work is that I know I'm good at it. It's nice also to be paid well, and as an apprentice to be learning new things. I still think about building my own home in the woods. And when I buy a book or magazine to read about owner-built homes, it's great to know I really can do it myself.

Maggie O'Neill POLICEWOMAN

When I talk to schoolchildren about my work, two questions always pop up. The children want to know if I carry a gun (I must, at all times, but I've never had to use it). And they wonder if I give tickets, like a metermaid (I don't). I've worked in most areas a policewoman can, but my favorite is the Youth Division. In fact, it's what attracted me to police work.

I had majored in psychology in college and was thinking of going into social work or teaching retarded children. I was trying to decide where to start and which field to enter. One day, while visiting some policewomen friends who worked in the Youth Division, I realized they were doing just what I wanted to do as a social worker—helping kids in trouble. So I signed up for the training program.

In our city, to qualify for training as a policewoman you must have at least a high school diploma, be at least five feet three inches tall, be at least twenty-one years old, and pass a preliminary (civil service) exam. Then you begin seven months of training with an exam at the beginning of each week. Subjects we learned were first aid, self-defense, criminal law, target practice, court procedures, traffic safety, sociology and a special law course at a local university. Lastly is two weeks of training on the job with an experienced policewoman or policeman.

The training was the hardest part of my work, but well worth it. When I graduated, my four children and my husband were very proud of me.

I've worked for a while in several different areas. In regular police patrol work I help watch over some part of the city in a patrol car with a policeman. I have also worked as a decoy in detective work. In everyday dress rather than uniform, a decoy can help uncover crimes without being recognized as a policewoman. A patrol car is always waiting nearby and I can signal when I need help.

In my favorite area, the Youth Division, we work with boys under seventeen and girls under eighteen who are either suspected or guilty of an offense, or who are victims of an offense. We try to find missing children (and adults) and we help children who are

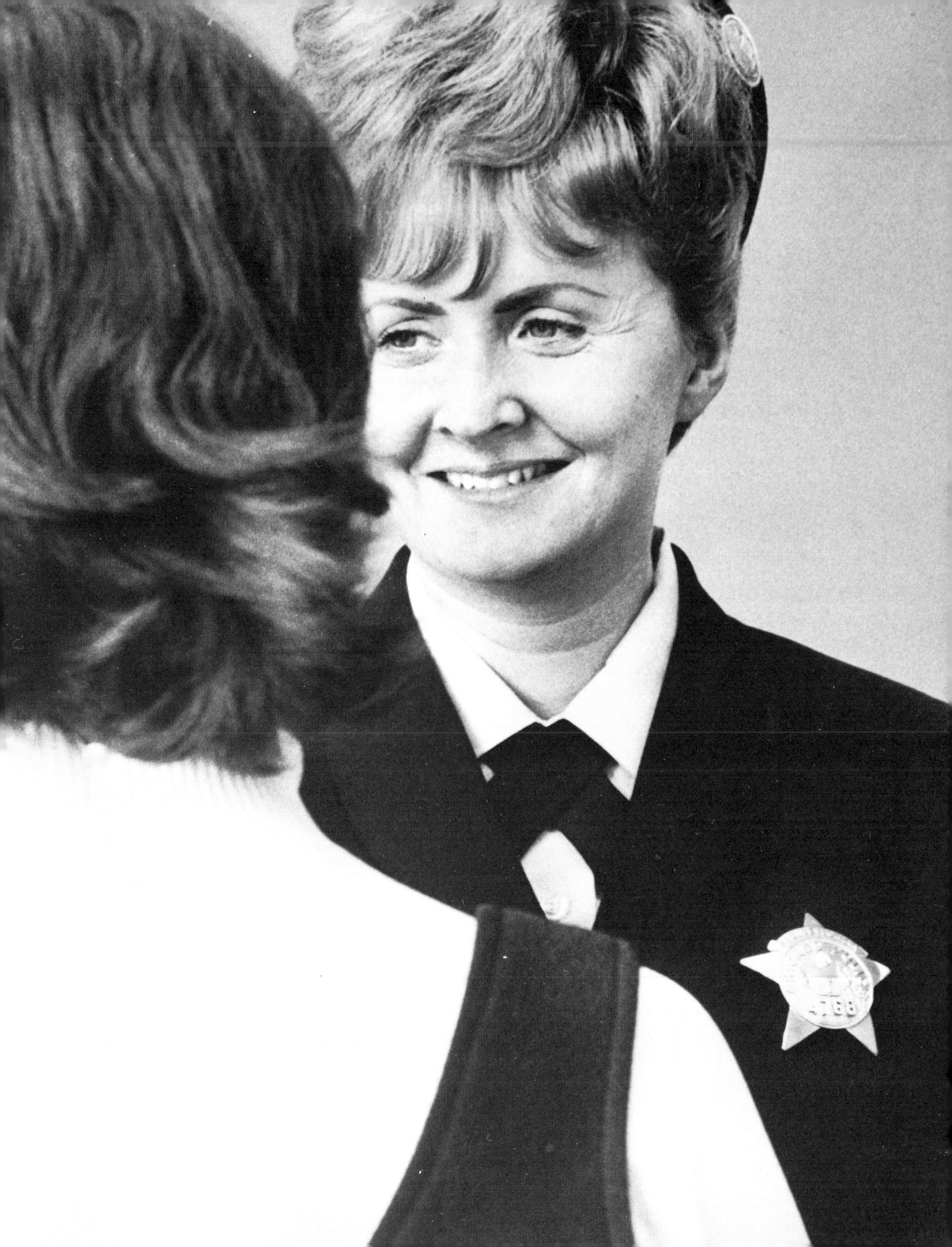

in trouble. When a child gets into trouble we first talk to his or her family, try to find out why the child did whatever he or she did, and we follow up by checking with the family later on. If the problem can be solved without the child going to juvenile court, we put the child in touch with a volunteer or agency. Some agencies can councel child and family together. Some volunteers—doctors, lawyers, parents and clergymen—spend time with children who can't talk to their own parents.

The most satisfying part of my work is helping children who have no one to defend them, such as children whose parents abuse them. In one case, after going to court for an eight-year-old girl six times, I was successful in helping to get her placed in a foster home away from her parents. Both parents were alcoholics and both beat the child repeatedly, but no one would go to court for the child. I'm glad I could.

Another program I've worked on is an educational course offered at local high schools which runs for ten days, with a lecture each day. There is one on self-defense, four on narcotics education, one on arrest procedures and the rights of a citizen if arrested, one on laws, one on the role of the policeman and policewoman, and one day of questions.

If a girl is interested in police work, and her local school does not have such a program, she might visit her local police department, ask for whatever brochures they may have about policework, and talk to a policewoman there. Or she might write to the public information department of the police department in the nearest large city.

Jean Tremulis FLORIST

My father's backyard garden gave me my first interest in growing things. He let me help and sometimes let me plant things myself—my first try was radishes. You might say that my first flower arrangement was a bunch of tulip tops I took from his garden for my mother. After that, my father taught me that you must pick flowers so that they still have stems, instead of loping off their tops.

I was steered into a flower arranging school by my high school art teacher. She knew I was having trouble deciding what to do when I graduated. And she knew I had been good in art classes and that I loved flowers. So she suggested a local school of flower arranging.

At the school we learned to arrange flowers to suit the occasions for which people use them; weddings, parties and funerals, and for sending to friends in hospitals or on special occasions. We learned color, materials, and all the other details of arranging flowers.

These schools only take a few weeks' time, and they are a fast way of finding out if you like this sort of work. They're located in most large cities. Horticulture, or the growing of plants, is a separate study and is usually taught in colleges. Some knowledge of horticulture is good for a florist to have, but these days florists do not grow their own plants for their shops. They are grown by large wholesalers who sell them fresh each day to shops. Another way of learning about flowers and plants is through the hundreds of books on the subject. Every library has many such books, for it's a popular subject. And one can also learn the business by working part time in a florist's shop.

When I had finished my course at the school of flower arranging, the woman who ran the school called a florist she knew who needed someone to help in her shop. I soon met the florist's brother, who was helping her manage it. After a time, he and I married and started a shop of our own.

To run a successful shop, you need both skill at flower arranging and good business sense. I enjoy the flower arranging and my husband enjoys managing the business, so we pool our talents. We share the responsibilities and trade ideas back and forth. He will often have good ideas on arrangements, and I on management.

Our home is overrun with all sorts of plants and we really enjoy them. Several times a week we water them all, working together so that it won't take so long.

Each morning that our shop is open, we make a trip to the local wholesaler to buy flowers and plants. Many are flown from California, where flowers grow all year round. We see what looks fresh, or look for things our customers have requested. Then we take the plants back to our greenhouse, which we use mainly as a holding area, a place to keep plants fresh. The flowers we keep in a cool place.

The busiest time of the year is Christmas. Mother's Day and other holidays keep us busy too, as do last-minute calls. On one such call, a mother of the bride asked us to please rush over one more bridesmaid's bouquet. She had been so nervous about the wedding that she had told us to make only four bouquets instead of five. I got the materials together, and made the bouquet in the truck in which my husband rushed me to the church and the waiting bridesmaid.

When we send flowers that are ordered for special occasions, it's like passing on a message from one person to another. We've said *I Love You* to perhaps 100,000 wives for their husbands, and *I'm Sorry You're Sick* for many others.

We've found that men also like flowers when they're sick, especially the brighter colors, like red, yellow and orange. I enjoy making tiny arrangements for children who are hospitalized. When making an arrangement for a child, sometimes I tuck in a tiny paper bird and bird's nest among the flowers.

This sort of care can't be shown by a computer, so we can certainly be confident that our business won't be taken over by machines. A flower arrangement is an individual and delicate thing, and can't be made any other way than by hand.

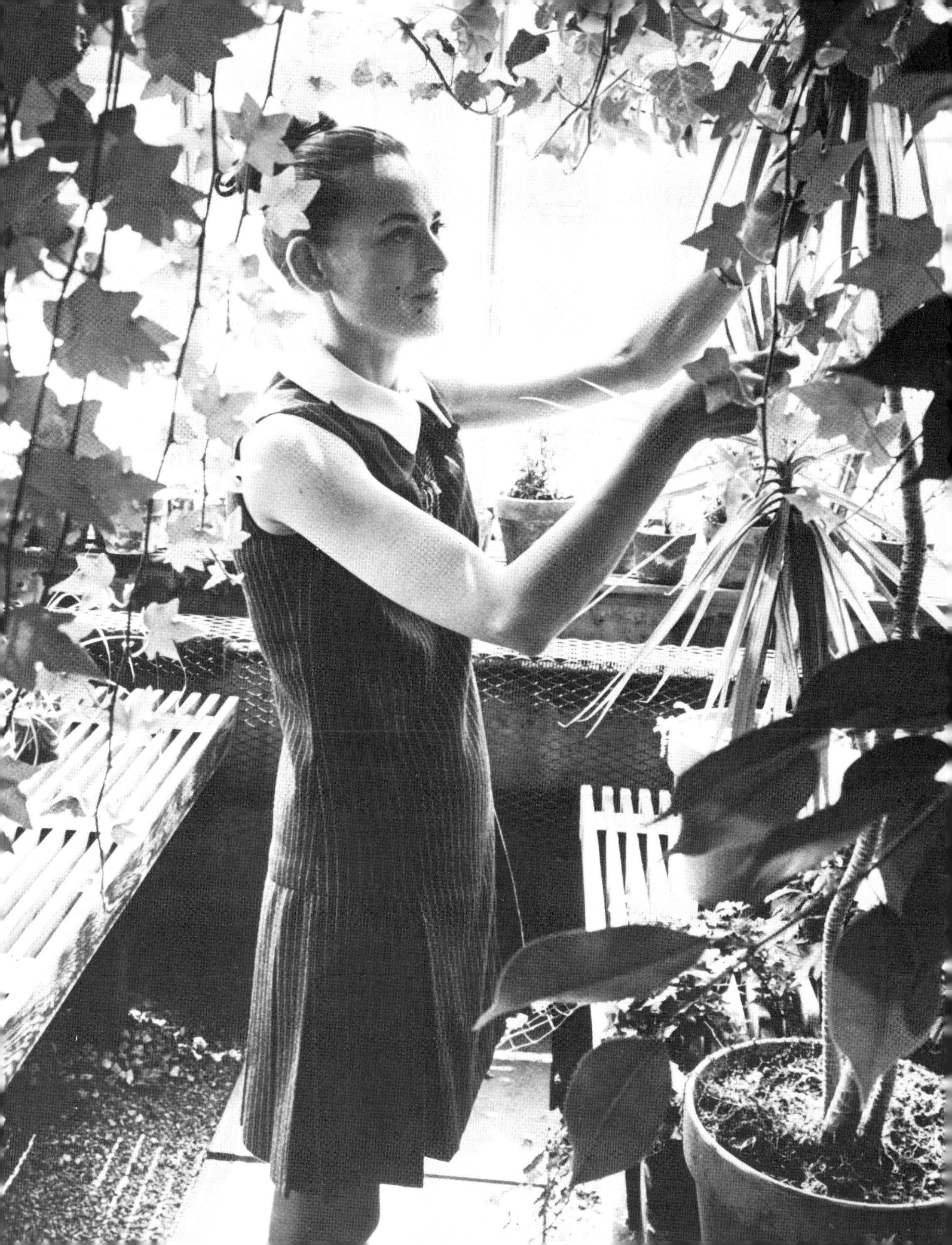

Margaret King   CAB DRIVER

I can remember when I was learning to drive—it was scary. I didn't know yet how to judge distance, and when a big truck came near it seemed like its wheels would just come right over me. I admired how cab drivers moved out just perfectly into the traffic and knew exactly where they were going.

Soon I learned to judge distance. I began looking ahead, stopped worrying about trucks and about what was moving on either side, and just took off. I took pride in driving well, for I had to wait until I had a car to learn to drive, and that was rather late in coming. When I finally learned, it was something I really enjoyed and still enjoy. I remembered how sharp those cab drivers had seemed—driving so well, and dressed so neatly in their uniforms—and I thought I'd like to do that myself.

Besides driving well, the most important thing a cab driver needs to know is the streets, and I knew the city well because I had lived in it for a long time. I knew all the main streets, and even the side streets, though I found some just a block long that I had never heard of before.

When I applied for the job, I was given a written test of the streets and main buildings. It's necessary to have a driver's license, and to have a good driving record. You must be at least eighteen, and of course, you should really like driving. After my written test, I was taken out in a cab and asked to demonstrate that I could drive it. Then I was given papers telling me what was expected of me, and I had the job.

When I first started working for the Yellow Cab Company and came home in a cab driver's uniform and hat, my neighbors congratulated me on joining the police force and my children said, "Mamma, you look just like a policewoman."

I soon found that what I liked best about this job was being outdoors, seeing how the city changes from season to season. Being in an office, you forget some of the landmarks, and can't watch each day of the changing seasons. Driving so much, there are places I've seen that I probably never would have seen in another job.

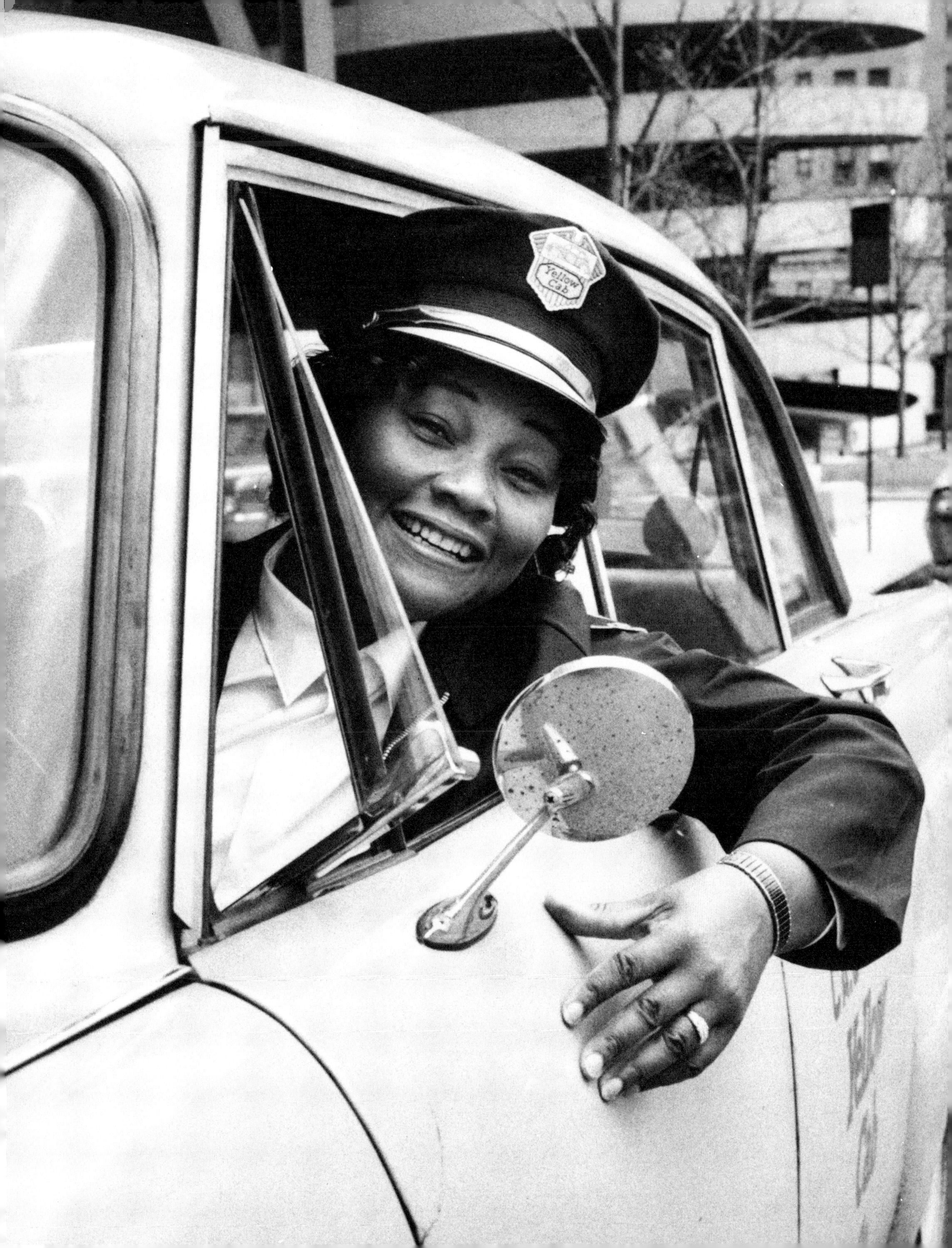
Yellow Cab

And I love all kinds of weather. I like to leave the window down in a fine rain, let it just blow in on me, and hold my arm out to catch the raindrops.

I enjoy meeting so many different people, too. Some I might not have met before this job, and I've learned a lot about how people behave. Some are interesting, some rushed, some pleasant, some funny and some think they're funny. Some are so pressed for time that they change clothes in the cab. Those who are in the greatest rush and say, "Get me there as fast as you can," are sometimes also in such a hurry that they forget to pay when get there. But for each one that doesn't pay, another overpays with a big tip—so it evens out. There are times when you meet a passenger who talks so nice, it makes you wonder how the one that just got out could have been talking so bad. It makes you think. Only one passenger really objected to having a woman driver and I laughed so at him that he stopped his fussing.

The only serious difficulty in this work is that it's sometimes dangerous to drive at night. But you have a choice, and I always choose to work days rather than nights. Generally, you use a cab during the day and someone else uses it at night. However, if you're a steady driver, you can get a regular cab with the same number each day. The pay isn't great, but with tips, it turns out pretty good.

Several of my children are grown and work in the city, and so does my husband. I wondered when I started driving a cab if I'd see them on the street as I traveled around. But it seemed that I was so busy watching for people signaling a cab, that I didn't recognize people I knew. Then one day I saw one of my daughters crossing the street to her office. I called out, "Young lady, be careful crossing the street like that, you might get yourself killed." She turned to see who it could be and was so surprised.

When I have a long drive near the end of the day, I sometimes go past my home to tell my two little children I'll be home soon, and they always want to come along. You can't take anyone along unless they pay or you pay for them. So I'll have to pay their fares one of these days and take them for a ride, because they really think it's fun.

I guess I know how they feel. I like to drive even though I do it for a living. Out in the countryside on a long drive, with the fresh air and the sun shining, you just seem to want to drive forever. At least, that's how it is for me.

Joyce Ginter REALTOR

When I was a little girl, my father had a business next door to a real estate agency. The realtor used to let me and my twin sister sit at the desks in his office sometimes. We would scribble on scrap paper and pretend to be answering phones and helping him sell houses. I liked the idea of getting people and homes together. Today my twin sister and I are both realtors—but not in the same city, which might confuse people.

As a realtor I help people sell and buy buildings of all kinds, but especially homes. A man who wants to sell his home may come to my office and ask me to help him find a buyer. When people come to me looking for a house to buy, I show them this man's home, if it seems right for them, as well as many others so they can choose. Then I help both buyer and seller work out the financial and legal matters that must be carried out whenever property is sold.

I began my training by working as a saleswoman in a real estate office. Then I became a real estate broker, which meant, among other things, that I was responsible for supervising other salespeople and helping run the office. Finally I became a realtor, which means I belong to local, state and national associations of real estate boards. Each state has a different law, and in my state both a broker and realtor must be licensed. Along the way I took a sixteen-week course at the state university, passed the university's exam and the state exam.

I met my husband when we both were brokers for another agency, and when we became realtors we both quit and started our own agency together. We've managed well so far by running our business and family together. The children help with housework and my husband and I cooperate in caring for the children. One of our daughters works at the agency in the summers and wants to be a realtor too.

The greatest satisfaction in my job is seeing a buyer get a home that is exactly right for him or her. What people need from a home is different in each case and it takes creative thinking to fit the home to the person. As a realtor my hours are my own and with five children it's great to be able to make appointments when

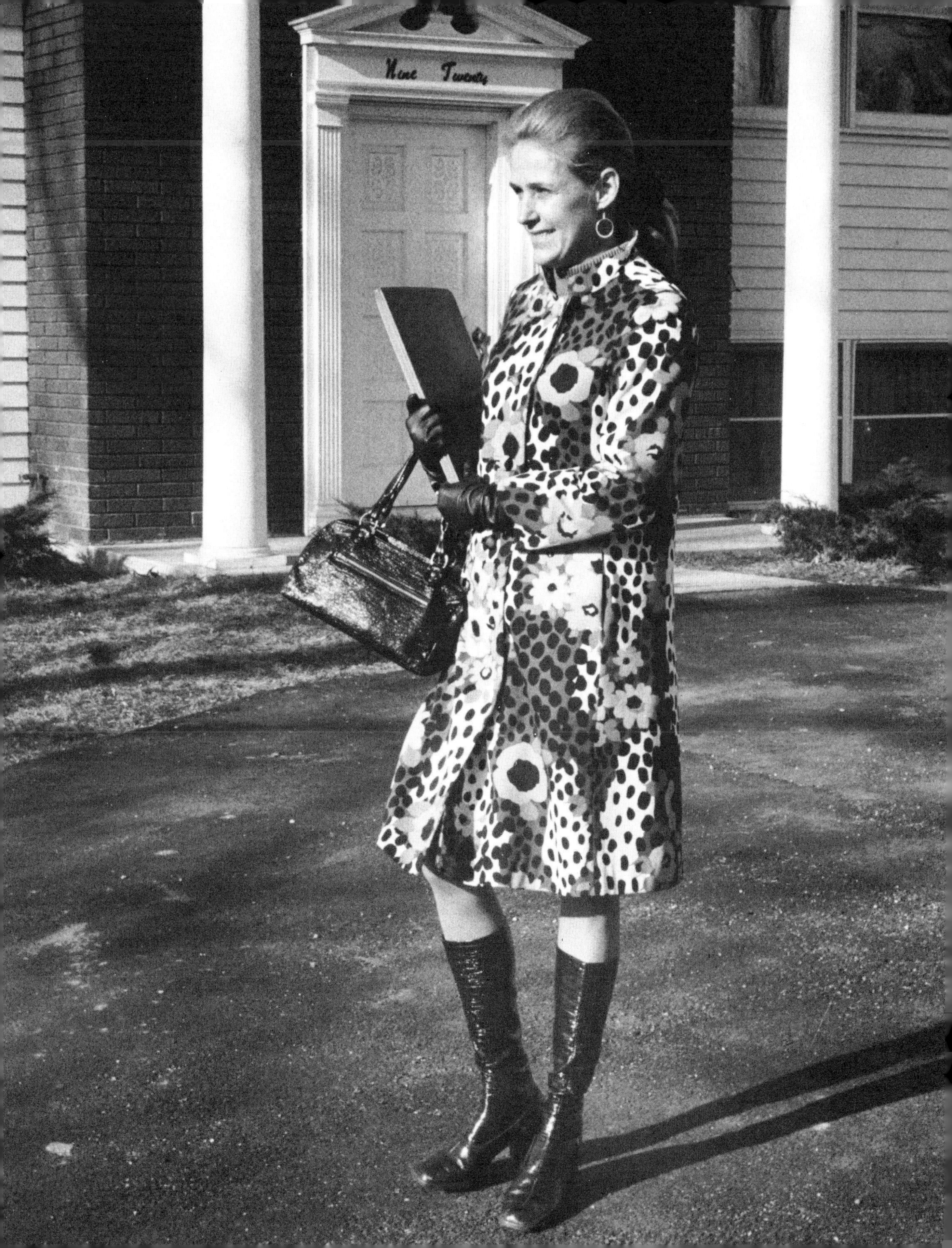
Nine Twenty

they are convenient for me. You are paid exactly what you are worth. If you work hard you make very good money, if you work harder, you make more. I like to be outdoors too, and showing homes to buyers lets me get out every day.

    A girl who is interested in this field might visit a local real estate office, or work in one for a summer. She could also ask to go along when someone she knows is shopping for a house and try to imagine which one will be chosen.

Mary Ann Goold TELEPHONE REPAIRWOMAN

When I graduated from high school, I needed a job right away. I saw a sign in the window of the telephone company that said operators' jobs were available, but after working as a telephone operator for just five months, I realized it was not the job for me. I hated staying in the same place all day and doing the same thing. What I liked was mechanical work and being active and outdoors. But I didn't see any women working at mechanical or outdoor jobs in the telephone company.

During a telephone strike, however, I noticed that women supervisors had worked in a department called "frames" which is a very mechanical area. They were nicknamed frame-dames. During a strike, emergencies must be handled, so telephone service is continued by those who are not on strike—the bosses. The women supervisors worked in frames during this strike, and the men worked at the outside jobs.

I realized that there were no women in frames or repair because none were asking. So I told my supervisor how I felt and asked her if I could apply for a job in frames. I had a very good supervisor at the time and she got me down there right away. I passed the test and got the job.

The test I took had little English or math; it was mainly an IQ type test of mechanical abilities and the aptitude for recognizing patterns and differences within patterns.

Frames are where you hook up the dial tone, toll equipment and other facilities needed in telephone use. Cables go from here outside and underground beneath the central office. You might imagine picture frames with wires that act to connect your phone—like each key of a piano is connected with a wire inside the piano, each striking at a different place.

From frames I was promoted to installation and from installation to repair, which is what I like best. Repair work can involve straight line, cable or aerial work. Cables are located underground in manholes or on poles. Straight line is that line which connects directly with a telephone, which sometimes needs repair when someone gets angry and pulls the cord from the wall. And aerial lines are those in the air, which we must repair when trees fall on them, squirrels get at them, or other such damage occurs.

My training for installation and repair work was given in a large actual work field inside a building. It's a special training program for all installers in which you climb poles and actually use the equipment. It's a learning-by-doing method. You work at your own speed, individually and on your own, but there are instructors there who give you work assignments and help you when you make a mistake. You're given a booklet which outlines each procedure and you follow its directions. I was not familiar with some of the tools, and had to ask many questions at first, but soon began learning more quickly. One supervisor kept trying to help me by telling me everything before I could do it. He meant well, but he was keeping me from learning by helping me too much. I asked for a different supervisor and soon was through the course.

There are many things I like about this work. Most of all I like doing mechanical work. I loved making model cars when I was a girl, and have always been good at such things. It's satisfying to do work that I know I can do well.

It's interesting, when installing phones or repairing phones in customers' homes, to meet them in everyday situations. Seeing customers you deal with in their own homes is much different than dealing with them in a shop or office.

I also enjoy being outdoors, seeing the seasons change and noting the new developments in the area. I like catching glimpses of birds, squirrels and rabbits.

There are a few frustrations to the job, naturally. No equipment can ever be absolutely perfect, and mistakes have to be met without getting upset. Sometimes on a pole I'll come upon a wasps' nest, and need to get out the spray we use to get rid of them.

But the satisfactions are greater than the frustrations. Most of all I enjoy the constant movement of people and life around me and the fact that I am using my mind to solve practical problems. When I fix a telephone that's been out of order, and the customer can use it again and is happy about it, that's an accomplishment I can actually see.

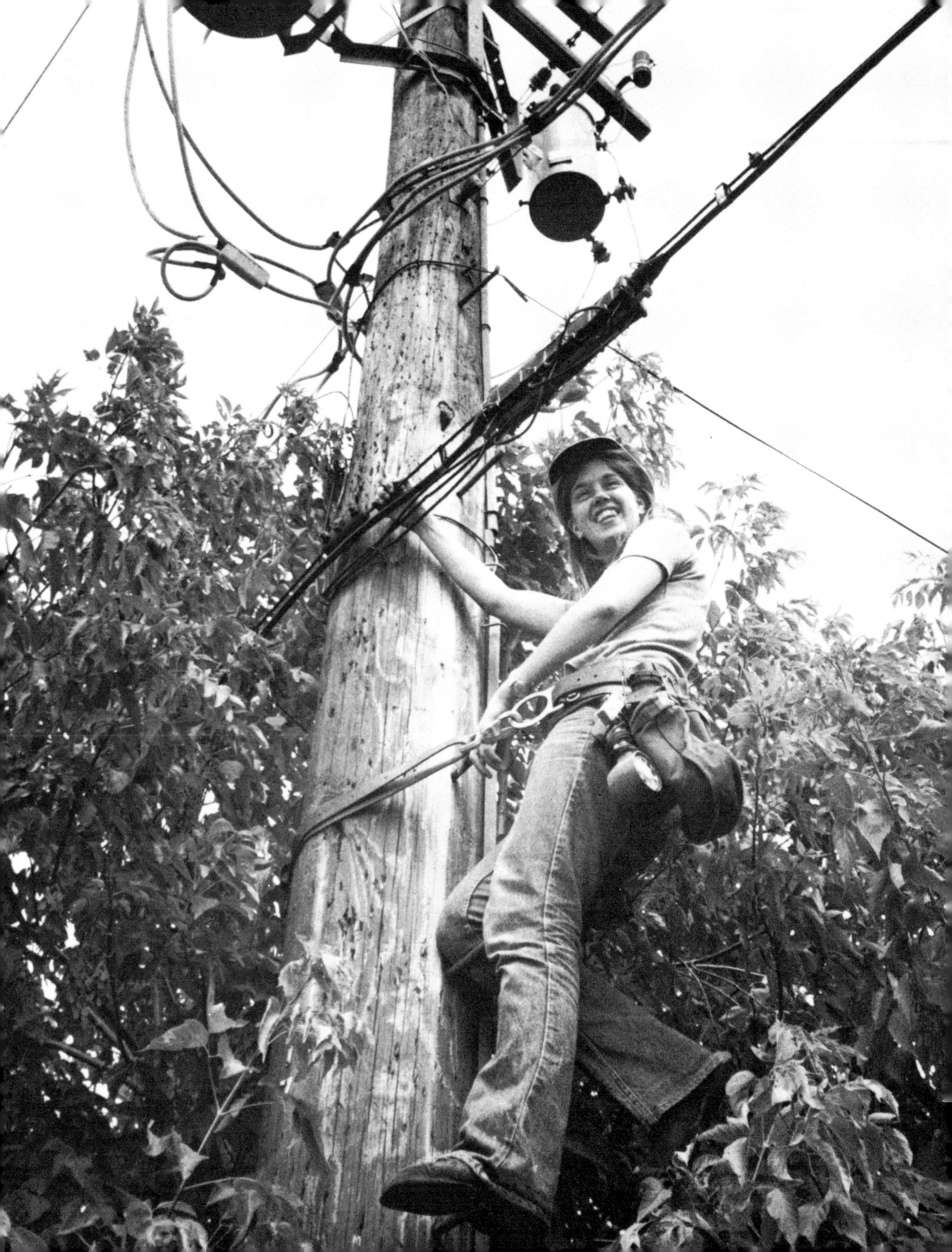

COMMERCE & GOVERNMENT

Patsy Takemoto Mink CONGRESSWOMAN

It was quite by accident that I got interested in partisan politics. I had started my practice of law in Hawaii. As a lawyer I was interested in social issues, but my notion of politicians was that they were self-serving people who were not interested in people's real problems. Some of my friends cajoled me into going to a political meeting one afternoon. It turned out to be a planning session for a political party's platform for the 1954 convention. A platform states the issues a party is concerning itself with, and I found that they were seriously dealing with social concerns, issues that people were really interested in. These people were not even running for office themselves but were trying to work at social change through politics. It was a very illuminating experience, and before I knew it, I was so deep into politics that it was practically my whole life.

Finding my way had been a complicated process before that. As a child I had wanted very much to be a doctor because it seemed to be the way to serve mankind. I admired my family physician very much. He was never too busy to say something nice when you were feeling bad; he really cared for people. But as I grew older it seemed that there must be other, perhaps more important, ways to serve mankind. As a doctor I could only help one person at a time, and only in a physical way. And this didn't seem to be enough.

One of the experiences that made me feel this way was my junior year in college. I had been studying zoology, thinking about being a doctor, when my father sent me to the mainland United States for my junior year. This affected me a great deal. I saw a bigger, more complicated world than I had known in Hawaii; I experienced racial prejudice for the first time, I became aware of many different social problems, and saw that changing the ethical basis on which society existed was more important to me than curing physical sickness.

When I returned to college in Hawaii, I began taking more courses in philosophy and religion, and thinking about how to use my life. So when I graduated, I wanted to help people, but I wasn't prepared for anything. I had a major in zoology and a minor in

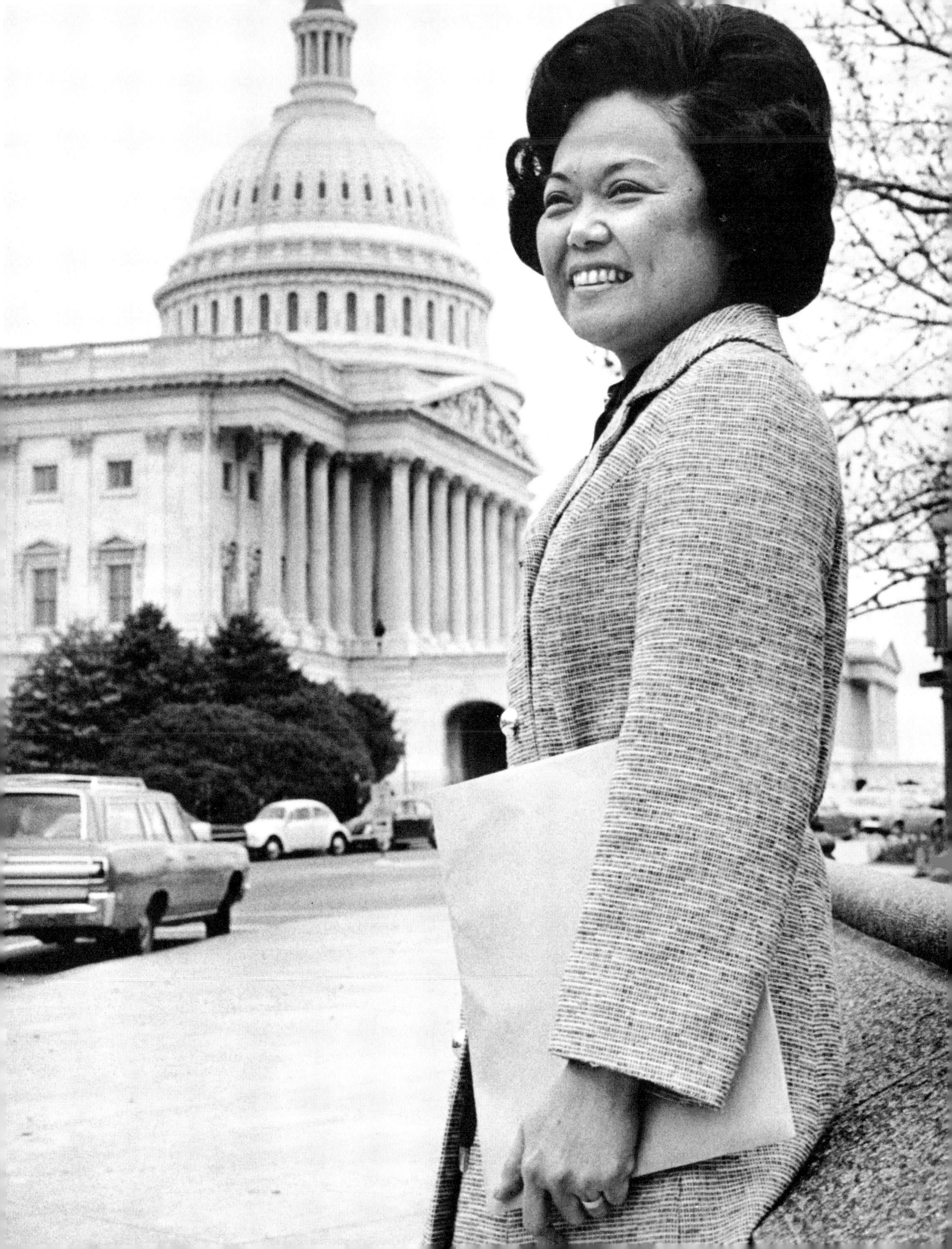

chemistry and physics, but the only jobs I could get at that time were washing bottles, working in photographic laboratories, and testing pineapples. So I was quite disillusioned, and took a job in an art academy as a typist. It seemed like a calming atmosphere and I needed time to think. By the end of the summer, I felt I was in such a rut that I had to snap myself out of it and make up my mind. So I analyzed that, the thing I wanted most right then was to be independent, a free spirit. It dominated my thinking that with a professional degree I could be on my own. The only profession where I could also deal with people's problems was law.

I chose the University of Chicago, not really knowing whether I would like it or not, but I found the first year extremely exciting. The whole approach at U. of C. was so unique—it didn't really present the law as what I had anticipated it to be. I had thought it would be a dry, case-by-case presentation of statutes and laws. Instead, the first year was a sort of social, philosophical approach to the entire institution of law.

Law turned out to be a very useful background for politics, and for women it is especially so. It gives you an instant credibility . . . since you have to fight the notion that some people have, that women don't understand laws and government, and since you have to struggle to prove that you have some ideas that should be considered. If you have a law degree, you can just skip that phase. You are respected because no one can question whether you understand the law: you are a lawyer, after all.

I've been a member of Congress now for eight years, as a Representative from the State of Hawaii. Before that I was a member of the Territory of Hawaii House of Representatives and Senate, and when Hawaii became a state, I was a member of the State of Hawaii Senate. In my present job as State Representative, I represent the people of my state by focusing attention on problems that exist in my state as well as in the nation. I project these concerns in the kind of bills which I sponsor, and the kind of bills I vote for when Congress is in session.

In a typical day I get up early, read several newspapers (those from Washington and Hawaii of course, and others that are opinion makers). When I get to my office I handle the mail, much of it questions and requests from people in my state. Then I attend to committee work and Congress goes into session at 12 noon.

Much of my committee work has been on education and labor committees. The most satisfying work recently has been help with child care for working mothers. It's been gratifying to see support for that program develop through five years time. At first there was very little interest in it and almost a hostility toward it; now it has finally gained majority support in the Congress.

Another bill I'm greatly interested in is one I recently introduced on the education of girls. I feel there is a need to change the whole philosophical approach towards the education of girls. Even with equal rights, girls will miss some opportunities until attitudes are changed. It is those attitudes that make up the life experience of a girl. For example, I was lucky in this regard. I don't know if this is true generally in Hawaii, but it was like this for me. I was never told by a teacher that there was any area of study that girls shouldn't be interested in. From first grade on, my teachers never questioned my use of my energies; whatever I wanted to do, they were always there to give advice on how to do it or how to do it better. My parents were never unenthusiastic or condescending. And my brother never told me I could not play baseball with him because I was a girl. No one ever said, "Girls don't do that." When I ran for student body president in high school, no one mentioned that a girl had not run for that before. This is how it should be. But when my daughter wanted to run for class president in school, she was told that office was for boys. That is how it should *not* be.

A girl who is interested in politics can find many things right in her own community to get started on. She can get involved in working on the local level for issues that she cares about. You don't even have to belong to a political party to be involved. There is a wider opportunity these days, with groups like the Common Cause, Ralph Nader's group, and the various environmental groups. These are all citizens' groups, not political parties. Political science courses are helpful in the study of political history, but your own active efforts are the best teacher. One of my hardest tasks is convincing peope about the importance of active participation. So many people are apathetic or cynical, they don't believe they can do anything about the world they live in through politics and they are wrong.

   Within an elective office, a single person can do even more for the issues that concern her. Public office is like a podium, from which you can speak for your constituents on the problems and issues that concern them. You can stir a large group of the public and focus their attention on the problems of the people you represent, even though you are only one.

Carol Ovitz COMMODITIES BROKER

On a commodities exchange, large amounts are traded in such things as corn, wheat, silver, plywood, eggs, soybeans and pork bellies. There is a great deal of action, shouting, gesturing, running to telephones, buying and selling. And yet one does not see the corn, wheat, silver and so forth in the commodities exchange where they are traded. It's all done on paper. A large manufacturer of bread, for instance, will have a trader in the commodities market make bids on the entire wheat crop of some large farm, even before the wheat has grown.

In the stock market, buying and selling is done in shares of public companies. You may buy so many shares of the telephone company, for example, but you are not buying the telephones themselves. In the commodities market, however, you are buying an actual commodity, such as corn.

I first became interested in the commodities market through a summer job as a research assistant in a brokerage firm. Brokers act as advisors and agents in financial matters such as the buying and selling of stocks and commodities. While I was working in the research department, someone got sick in the commodities department, and I was asked to help out there. It seemed like the most exciting kind of financial market for it moved very fast and was directly affected by such various things as weather and politics. There was a corn blight not long ago, in which crops across the country were ruined, and the first news of it caused feverish activities in the commodities market, for when something is scarce, its price goes up. Those who would need large quantities of corn in their business were anxious to be sure they had it.

In this business, fortunes can be made and lost so fast that one has to be alert. Not only are you dealing with big money, but with other people's money. It's often necessary to use psychology to guess how a piece of news will affect the market, so that you can buy and sell for your clients in such a way as to make money for them, and not lose it. Even so, there are times when things happen so fast that everyone is winning or losing together, and there's not enough time to buy and sell so as to avoid being one of the losers. It keeps you thinking fast.

When I graduated from college, I went back to the firm where I had spent my summer and I asked them if they were willing to train a woman as a broker. They never had before, but they were willing and I began.

It's not a field one can learn from how-to books; one must be trained *on* the job. I learned by taking buy and sell orders over the phone, reading news tickers, listening to other brokers, talking to customers and reading reports and newspapers.

When I had become established as a broker and promoted to assistant vice-president of my firm, I decided the next logical step was to apply for membership in the Board of Trade, the largest commodities exchange in the world.

This is the place where the actual trading goes on; the place where I spoke of so much shouting, gesturing, running to telephones, buying and selling. It's an enormous place, and the trading floor is an expansive room with a three-story ceiling. Across the floor are numerous areas called pits, which are octagonal sets of stairs which rise up and then down, forming pit areas. Each one is the trading space for a different commodity—wheat, corn or whatever. The traders in that commodity all stand together around the pit waiting for the opening bell. As soon as it rings, they begin to trade—by shouts and hand signals. Their trades are recorded on large boards that surround the room, and orders are carried back and forth to them by runners who beat a path fom the pits to the telephones. The place is a storm of activity and flying scraps of paper for several hours until the closing bell, when all is quiet again until the next day.

When I applied for membership in the Board of Trade, there had never been a woman member there, just as there had not been at my firm before I came. Many of the members thought I might be joining just to prove something. But they soon realized that I was as sincerely interested in the field as they were, and liked the place just as much as they. Since the commodities market was my life work, I wanted to be part of it to the fullest extent. And being a part of the biggest exchange would certainly help.

The study of many subjects, and the avid reading of news-

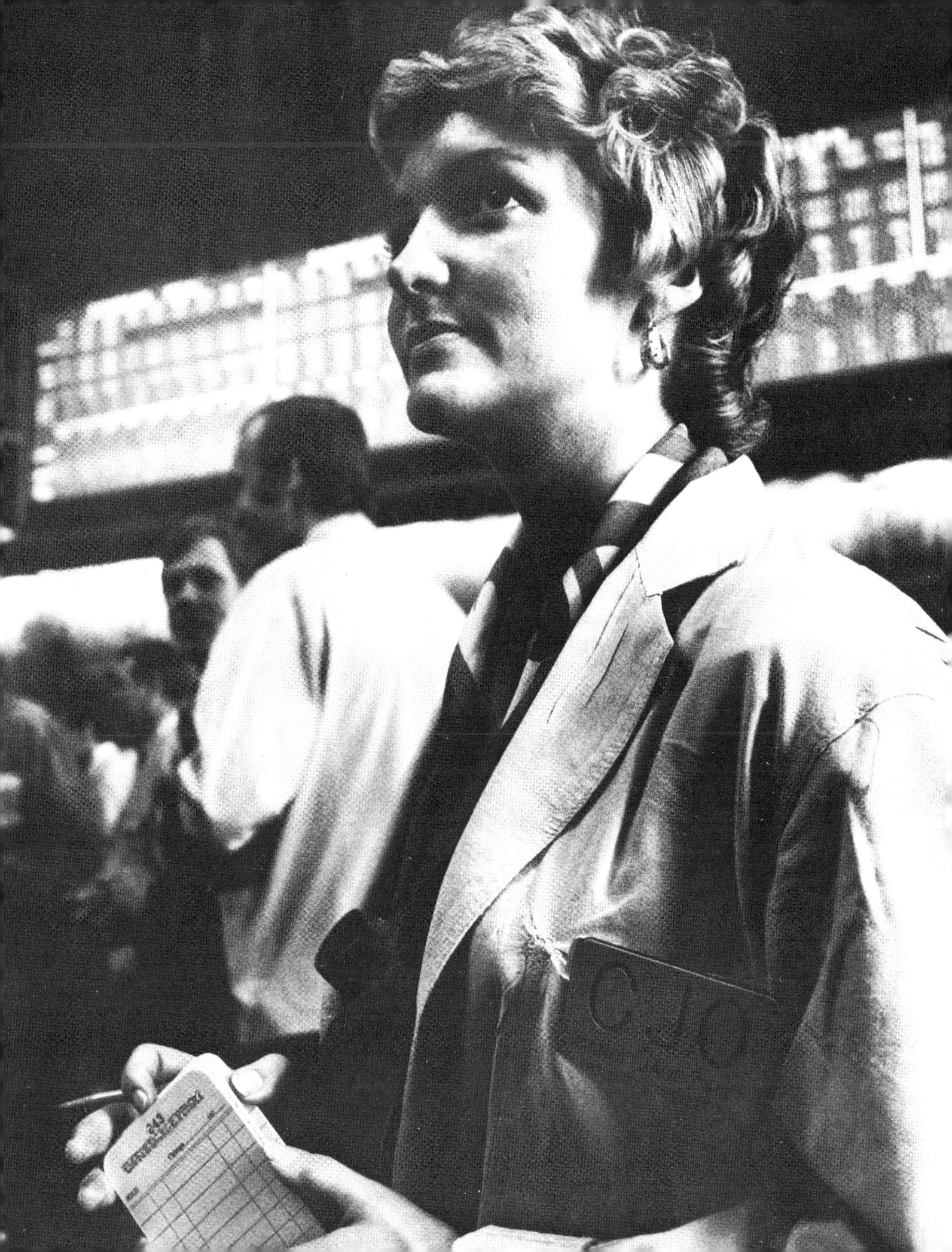

CJO
243

papers and business publications can be helpful in this field. But one must learn how it works by being on the scene. Breaking-in jobs include research jobs such as I had my first summer in the business, and "runner" jobs in the large exchanges. There are exchanges only in a few large cities, however, while brokerage firms are more widely scattered.

    I'm happy with the field I've chosen, even on days when the phones never stop ringing. It's no nine-to-five job, and it's different every day.

Francine Dickey ACCOUNTANT

I help businesses and people with a problem everyone has—money. As an accountant, I help them figure out where their money goes to and comes from, how it can best be used and invested, and also help with another chore everyone has—taxes.

Numbers weren't always as much fun for me as they are now. In school I hated arithmetic and got bad grades in it. I thought numbers were dull. One summer, I took a job as a bookkeeper, which meant keeping accounts of numbers. I thought I'd hate it and only took the job because it paid more than secretarial work. To my surprise, I found that when numbers stood for real money, real people, and real problems to analyze, I was fascinated by them.

Many people think all that is involved in accounting is the mechanics of adding and subtracting numbers. The true nature of accounting is not these mechanical routines but the analytical process that makes numbers come alive. Numbers meant more to me when I began to see them as representing the time, money and human effort that goes into a business. I suddenly became much better at math, and went on to college to take the math, tax, English, and other courses I needed to be an accountant.

Another wrong idea I had, that accountants were dusty, fussy and old, was changed when I got my first job. The people were interesting, young and fun to work with. I work in a public accounting firm that handles the business of large companies. Some private businesses hire their own accountants, which means that you can work in a wide variety of firms without changing careers. Some accountants run their own offices or work right in their homes on small business accounts and taxes.

Each state has different rules regarding accounting. You can write to your State Board of Public Accounting to find out what the requirements are. In some states a college degree is required to become a public accountant, but not to work as an accountant for a company. In others you can learn by working for another accountant until you know enough to pass the state exam. In all states you must take some sort of test to become a CPA—certified public accountant.

There have been some unexpected advantages to me in my choice of a career. One is that I've been able to make math a little more interesting for my daughter. Like me at her age, she dislikes math, but I give her problems to work out where real money is involved, like figuring out our grocery bills, or deciding how much she'll need for a new record she wants.

Another thing I like about accounting is that accountants will always be needed no matter how many computers a company has, because creativity is needed to make judgements, even with numbers. And computers can only go so far in giving analysis or advice.

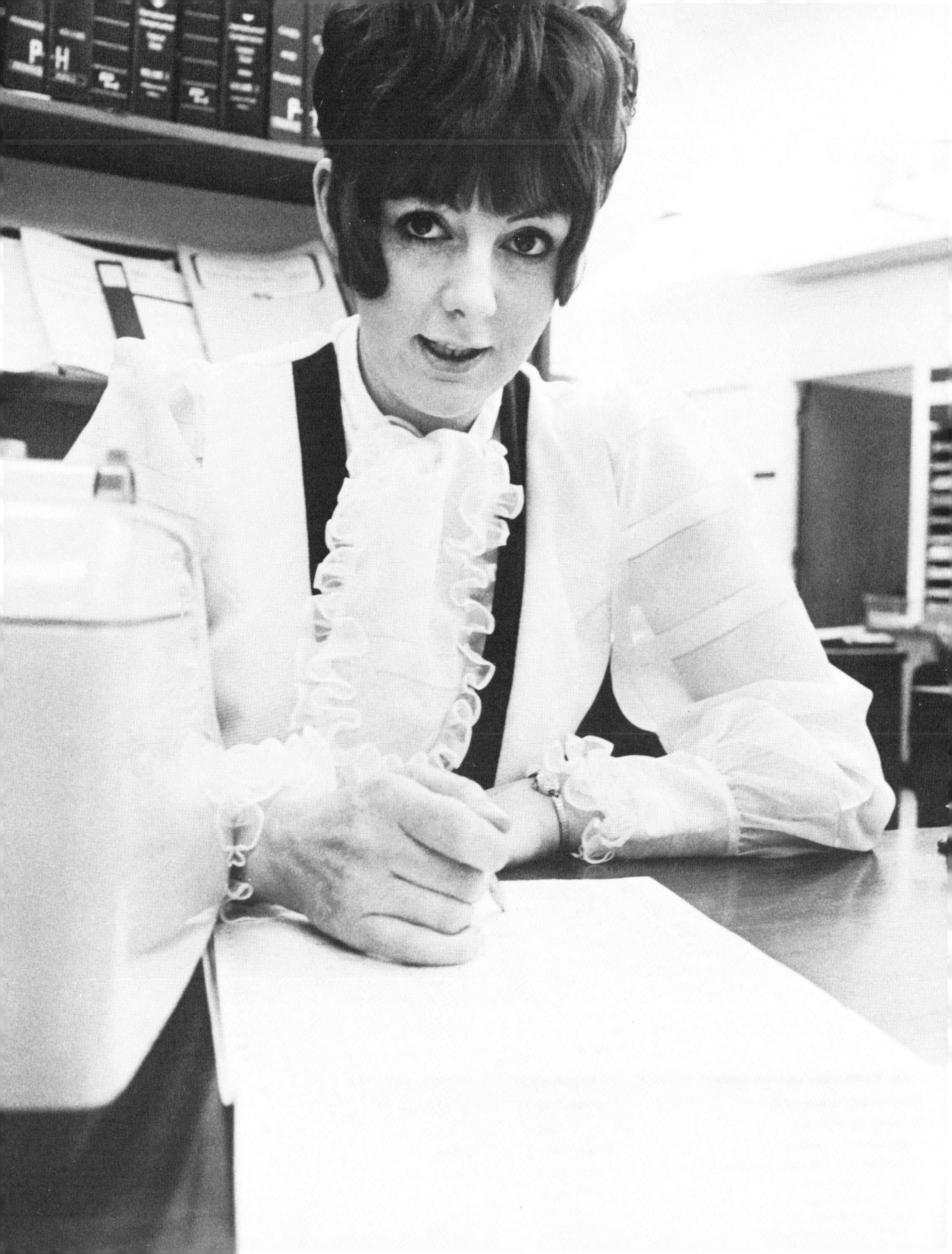

Elizabeth McLain CITY PLANNER

I lived on a farm when I was young, which gave me many opportunities to do what I liked best—build things. My brother and I built fences, chicken coops and all the small buildings needed on a farm, and still had space to design others just for fun.

Very early I began seeking information to find out what fields there were in which one could build or participate in building. I took books home from the library on architecture and engineering, asked questions, and took aptitude tests. While I was in high school there were seminars and conferences for girls on careers. One on engineering was sponsored by the Society of Women Engineers. I found out I'd need all the math and science courses I could get. When I graduated, I was sure what I wanted to study in college.

I chose the field of civil engineering and city planning. Civil engineering attracted me because it is the building arm of engineering, and involves construction of many different public works: buildings, roads, transit lines, sanitation facilities, bridges, dams, canals and harbors. City planning seemed like an exciting field because it involves the development of urban areas. A city planner puts down the lines that make a city work. He or she decides where roads should go, so they can service people who live in an urban area and get them from home to work, from home to shopping, and so forth. A planner decides where waterlines and sewer lines should go, and helps with the problem of getting waste taken away from industrial areas. Plans are also needed for neighborhoods, parks and schools—all calculated on the basis of how many people live where. Planning includes zoning, regulations for developers, and all the social aspects of city living.

My job now is with a city planning commission. Some work is done in the office and some in the field. First we choose and check out sites. Then we must check on all work as it progresses, visiting the foremen on whatever projects are in progress, making sure everything is on schedule. Since a civil engineer supervises projects in which there are mechanical, chemical and electrial engineers, she or he must know something about each of these fields.

Mechanical engineering has to do with machines. Chem-

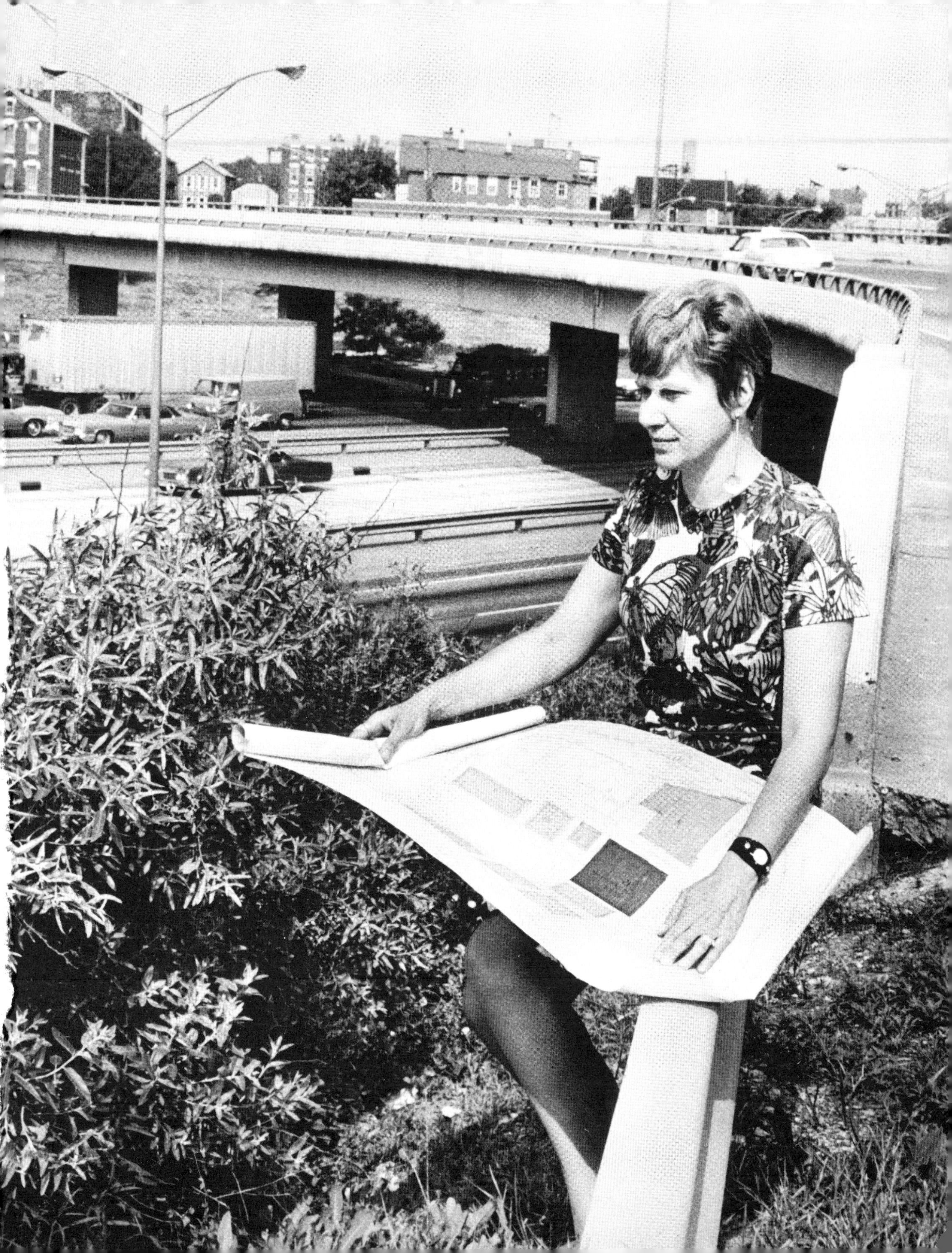

ical engineering applies chemistry to industrial processes. Electrical engineering involves electricity everywhere you find it. Civil engineering calls for more field work, while chemical and electrical engineering involve more work in the office.

One may specialize in any of these types of engineering. A degree in the field generally takes four or five years of college. Wisconsin, Georgia Tech, IIT and MIT are all good engineering schools, and a counselor can locate more for you. Jobs have been scarce recently for engineers, but no more so for women than for men. The job situation is expected to improve in the near future.

Jeanne M. Holm   BRIGADIER GENERAL

In World War II, it seemed that everyone was joining up—volunteering for the armed forces. Both my brothers had joined the Navy. And many women were just waiting for a law to be passed to permit women to join. The Army was the first to do this, so I joined the Army.

The training then, in 1942, was a make-over of the men's program. The Women's Army Corp had not yet found its own way. It was exciting to help in organizing this new part of the armed forces. We wrote our own programs and made training aids, and we developed our own curriculum for the eight weeks' training period. During this time I was the commander of a basic training company and then of a training regiment. After that I was commander of a WAC hospital company.

I decided to go to college on the GI Bill when I was released from active duty. During the Berlin crisis, I was recalled to active duty in the Army and decided that I would like transfer to the Air Force. It had just been created as a separate service.

Part of the attraction of the Air Force for me was the fact that I had always liked planes and flying. But more important, it was an entirely new service. Women would be part of the Air Force from its very beginning so there were no traditions to fall back on. The Air Force was coeducational from the start and had a clean slate. Women were to be promoted and used on an equal basis with men.

Then came a bad time. For a while, in the fifties, opportunities for women seemed to stagnate and this affected the Air Force as well as women in civilian life. Women in the Air Force had fewer jobs than before that were open to them, and the number of women serving on active duty was cut to about half. Things had to change.

One of the achievements I'm most proud of was working to change this situation. It helped that women everywhere in the 1960's were beginning to be more interested in the world around them and looking for a better choice of jobs. The Air Force recognized that women could do far more jobs well in the services than the clerk-typist and medical technician jobs they had been limited to during the 50's. As a result, all Air Force jobs were opened to women, except those that required extreme physical strength or those that involved active combat.

For example, Women in the Air Force cannot be pilots, co-pilots, or weapons controllers, but *can* be control tower operators, intelligence officers, space systems analysts, weather officers, chemists, photographers, veterinarians and doctors. Or they can work in missile and aircraft maintenance, logistics, avionics, personnel and administration, as well as other fields.

Partly as a result of this, plus equal pay and promotion, the numbers of Women in the Air Force have doubled in recent years. If this continues the ratio of women in the armed forces is going to be greater than ever. As we move forward, it may be that the Air Force will commission mostly people who have degrees that are needed rather than liberal arts degrees. I encourage girls to get their education first, aiming at practical applicable skills. A girl must have a high school diploma to apply for the Women in the Air Force and must be able to meet certain physical and mental requirements. There are also age requirements, and she must be of good moral character.

When a Woman in the Air Force marries, we make a special effort to keep husband and wife together, and in most cases we succeed. It's kept in mind when assignments are made, for a person in the armed forces may be assigned to places all over the world. If a woman wants to stay in the Air Force while she is pregnant and is willing to face up to the problems associated with child care, she can usually stay in. She must take her own leave when the baby comes, but we find that the average lost time is only 35 days. However, finding adequate child care is not the only problem. The woman must accept the fact that she and her husband are available for world-wide assignment. That's the difference between being a mother in the military life and as a civilian working woman. This may be the most difficult part of military life for a woman to cope with.

I'm glad I chose this life, however; I can honestly say that I've always had challenging jobs in interesting places. And I was

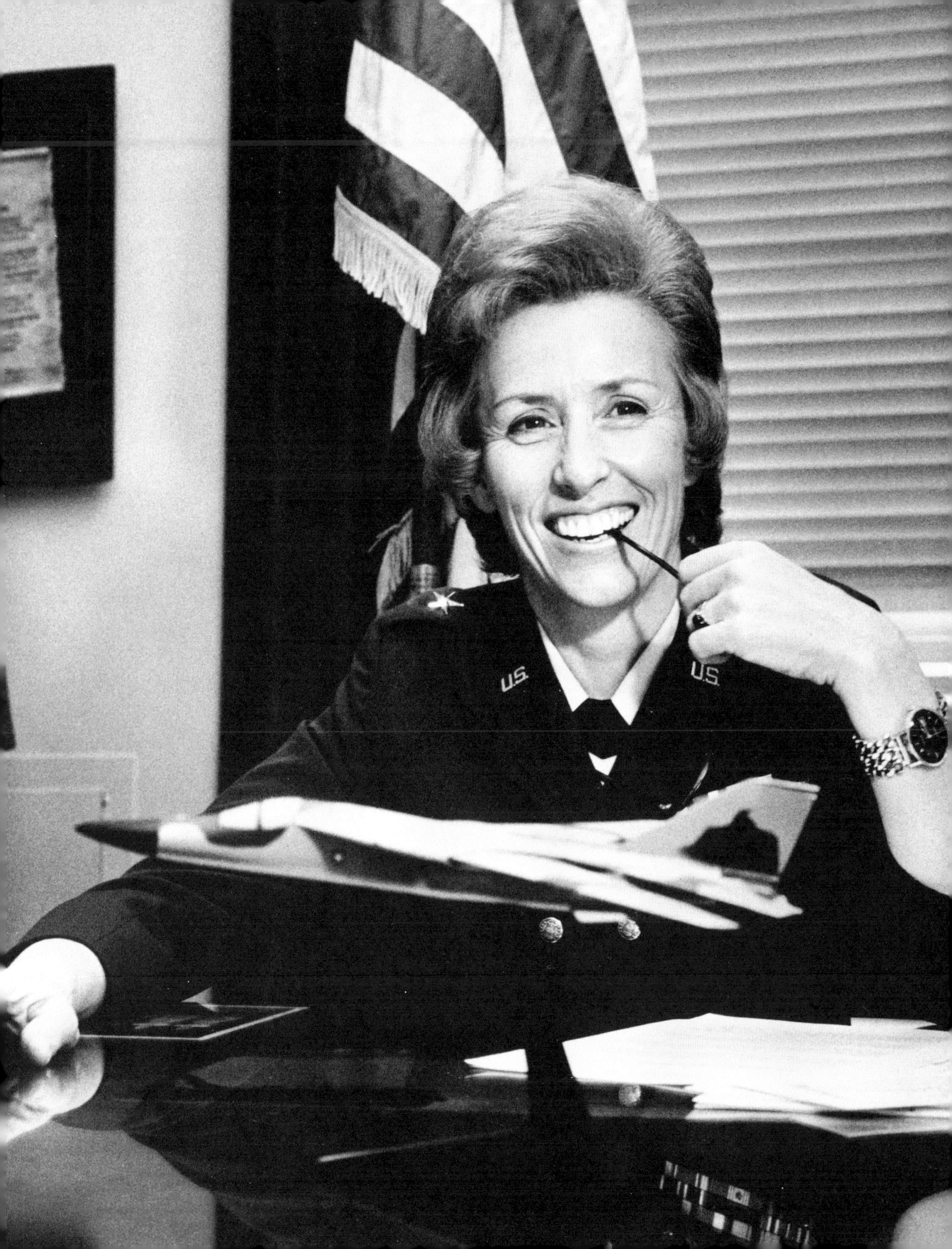
U.S.
U.S.

recently promoted to the rank of general. This makes me particularly happy since the Air Force did not have to be pushed by anyone to promote a woman to the rank of general. They did that on their own. I've never felt that I was held back because I was a woman. That doesn't mean that everyone has had this experience—in some ways I simply lucked out.

My most satisfying work so far has been in the position I now hold as Director of Women in the Air Force. Each general has a different job, and this is mine at the moment. I didn't expect it to be as fulfilling as it is; there are very few jobs, high up, where you can really see the results of what you do and have an impact on people. But this has happened in this job. We've been able to change the whole direction of Women in the Air Force, completely modify the uniforms, and update jobs.

My funniest experiences seem to come from reaction to the uniform. Some stare because they see few women generals. Others think that perhaps I'm an airline stewardess. Once, on a commercial airliner, a little old lady mistook me for the pilot. She jumped up and said, "If she's flying this thing, I'm getting off." It's a shame that people sometimes feel that way about women, but it was very funny at the time, and times are changing.

The passage of the Equal Rights Amendment raises some interesting questions. Women will be given equal rights, and perhaps equal duties. Let's hope that we never have to go back to the draft, but if we do, I would imagine that women, fifty per cent of the population, will not be overlooked. Although the law prevents them from active combat, there are thousands of other jobs in the services that they can do.

One of the things that first attracted me to the Air Force was my interest in planes. Amelia Earhart was my childhood idol, and though I couldn't afford flying lessons, I took all the ground school courses I could. Although the job of pilot is one of the few not open to me in the Air Force, I haven't missed it. I've flown millions of miles as a passenger, and when I want to pilot, I take a spin in my motorboat.

Jewel Lafontant LAWYER

My father was a lawyer, and his father before him. I enjoyed watching my father at work when I was a child, visiting his office and seeing him in court. In the summers, when I was old enough, I would help out in his office, and I, too, gradually became interested in law. After law school I went to work in a law firm, later became a partner in my present firm, and married another lawyer. My son often asked to come along with me to court when he was younger, and my daughter sometimes has worked summers in our law office and speaks of becoming a lawyer too. It certainly seems to run in the family.

My memories of my father's office are very pleasant ones. I taught myself to type so that I could help, and learned to do some of the research necessary in preparing briefs for court. A brief is a list of the facts a lawyer will need in court. One of my biggest thrills as a young woman was helping my father to prepare a brief in a case for the Supreme Court, the highest court in the country.

School had always been easy, so I found to my surprise that I really had to study hard in college. I picked Oberlin, and I took political science to prepare for law school and physical education for fun. Then it was on to law school. There I concentrated on two areas of interest—family law and constitutional law—and many of my cases have been in these two areas.

In family law, I deal with child custody, that is, who should care for a child when parents are divorced or absent. I also deal with family tax problems, trust funds and divorce. In constitutional law I deal with civil rights and fair employment cases.

My first job as a lawyer was with the Legal Aid Bureau, defending people who were being evicted from their homes. Many of my early cases involved civil rights. In one instance, I helped remove discrimination from the prisons by a court case in which I fought a prison policy that set aside certain jobs for white people only.

Not all of a lawyer's work is done in court. If I have a case I feel should not be won, I try to work out a settlement between the parties involved—out of the courtroom. In some cases there is no right or wrong, and in these cases it's best to settle out of court.

In some divorce cases I am able to help save the marriage and the case doesn't have to go to court at all. In other divorce cases I am sometimes able to help the parties involved from causing damage to each other or their children by too much battling in court.

There's much more involved in a divorce case than just the breakup of a marriage. A great deal of planning is involved for the welfare of the children, if there are children, or in the fair settlement of matters of property.

On a few occasions a case was won before my client and I even got to court. In one recent case a woman was suing her employers because of their refusal to promote her. They would not promote her because she was a woman. The employer argued that there was a state law that says women cannot work more than forty hours a week, and that the job this woman should have been promoted to involved more hours than that. A man who was not as well qualified as she had been promoted instead. Well, this law was made long ago and was supposed to protect women from working extremely long hours at heavy jobs. In today's world, however, such a law hurts a woman instead of helping because it keeps her from better jobs and better pay. Before we even went to court, the company realized the unfairness of the law and gave my client a better promotion than the one she was going to court over. So we won without going to court.

My practice now includes corporate law, which is law relating to businesses. When my husband and I were married, my father and I joined his firm, which specializes in corporate law.

I enjoy working with my husband within the same firm and at the same profession. We're both so busy at the office that we hardly ever see each other there. Where it really helps is at home because we understand one another's work and can talk over any problems we have in our work. Law is a demanding profession and it's an advantage to have a husband who understands that.

Corporate law is an interesting specialty, for businesses have a hand in running the country to a great extent. I did not expect to become directly involved in business, but recently I was asked to become a member of the board of directors of a major airline

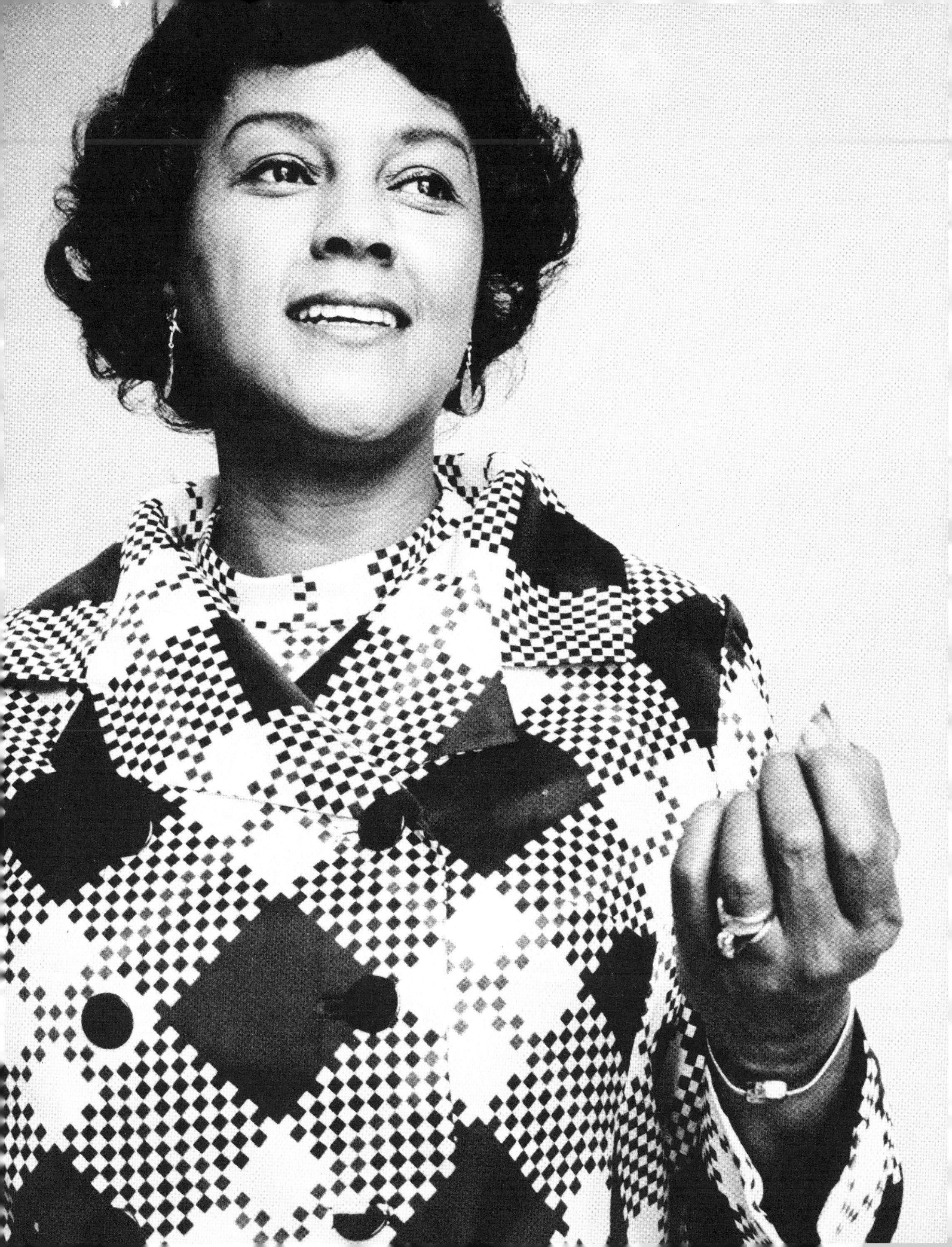

and also of a large food chain. A board of directors is chosen from community leaders and professionals whose knowledge might help the company in making business decisions. The president of a company is on the board, and some of the members belong to that company. Other members are from outside the company. Each is selected for some particular point of view he or she can bring to the board, and an outside point of view is often helpful. These boards decide what the company's policies will be, who should be hired or fired, what salaries should be paid, et cetera.

Lawyers are often asked to be on various boards, not only for their knowledge of law, but because of the belief that one who has gone through law school has shown that she or he has learned to think in an organized, disciplined way and can carry a project through. This makes that person's judgment valuable to businesses.

Many lawyers get interested in politics and I'm no exception. I was a delegate for the 1960 Republican Convention, traveled with Henry Cabot Lodge on the Civil Rights Commission, and later was appointed to the United States Commission on International Education and Cultural Affairs, and the National Council on Minority Business. I attended the 1972 Republican National Convention as a delegate at large. This time I was able to take my son, who is fourteen, so that he could watch some of the government processes he reads about in school.

Corporate law and government work have brought me increasing opportunities for travel, and for becoming experienced in international law. Last year I traveled to Africa for a client who wanted to set up a business there. The airlines board on which I serve occasionally meets in different countries, and a state department committee took me to the Philippines and Thailand.

To become a lawyer, one needs three or four years of college, followed by three years of law school. Some law schools have night classes, for those students who work.

There is less need now for lawyers in general practice and more for lawyers in specialized fields. Businesses are changing constantly and need lawyers in many of their dealings. Lawyers help them with tax and labor laws that have become more and more complex, and with new situations like cable television, computerization and changing relations with foreign countries. As different groups seek equal rights, there are more and more cases involving discrimination, which call for lawyers to represent the people involved. Even criminal law changes. Old laws are repealed and something that was once considered a crime ceases to be a crime. But at the same time new situations arise, calling for new laws.

Some of the special fields in law which a girl might consider are patent law, labor law, international law, corporation law, criminal law and tax law. There are a few courses available in the third year of law school in such areas as tax, labor, or corporation law. A person who studies engineering might go on for a degree in law and specialize in engineering law. But in most cases, one gets experience in a specialty by finding a place with a firm that practices that specialty. The law degree itself is meant mainly as a discipline, a way of thinking and learning how to think. It makes a good base for a career in business or government as well as for special areas of law, because it is a good general education. It holds you in good stead no matter what kind of career you aim for.

Jan Heise MARKETING EXECUTIVE

As a girl, the business world seemed to me like nothing more than a briefcase and a lot of problems. My father was a businessman and I imagined his work to be totally dull. I felt I'd like to work with people and I thought that the only fields where I could do that were nursing and psychology. So that's what I studied in college.

A part-time job one summer in a business office changed my thinking. I found business to be far from dull, and working with people in my office gave me ample opportunity to use the psychology I'd learned. I found that marketing was the most attractive field for me, so when I went back to college I changed my major to marketing. My background in psychology was very helpful to me in this field, for marketing is the study of what people buy, why they buy what they do, what products are needed and should be developed, how products should be presented, where they should be sold, and so on. As an executive in this field I must know how to deal with a wide variety of situations and different kinds of people in many parts of the country.

I started with a small consulting firm, then moved to a larger firm because of its broader scope. The products we help our clients with range from small supermarket items to the electricity produced by power companies. In a typical day, I start work at nine, meet in my office with colleagues, and plan the day. At ten I make phone calls to check on previous days' work and how it's developing. At ten thirty, I meet with clients to talk about their products. I find out all I can about what it is they have to sell and how they feel about it, which is what I need to know to decide what my firm can do for them. Then I have lunch, and after lunch I arrange for research on the problems that were discussed with the client that morning.

It's a challenging problem, deciding how a product should be sold; for what people want and what people will buy is something that varies from region to region. Tastes change too, and a product that might have been useful ten years ago might be useless today. The kind of package that a product has makes a difference too, and so does the way it's presented.

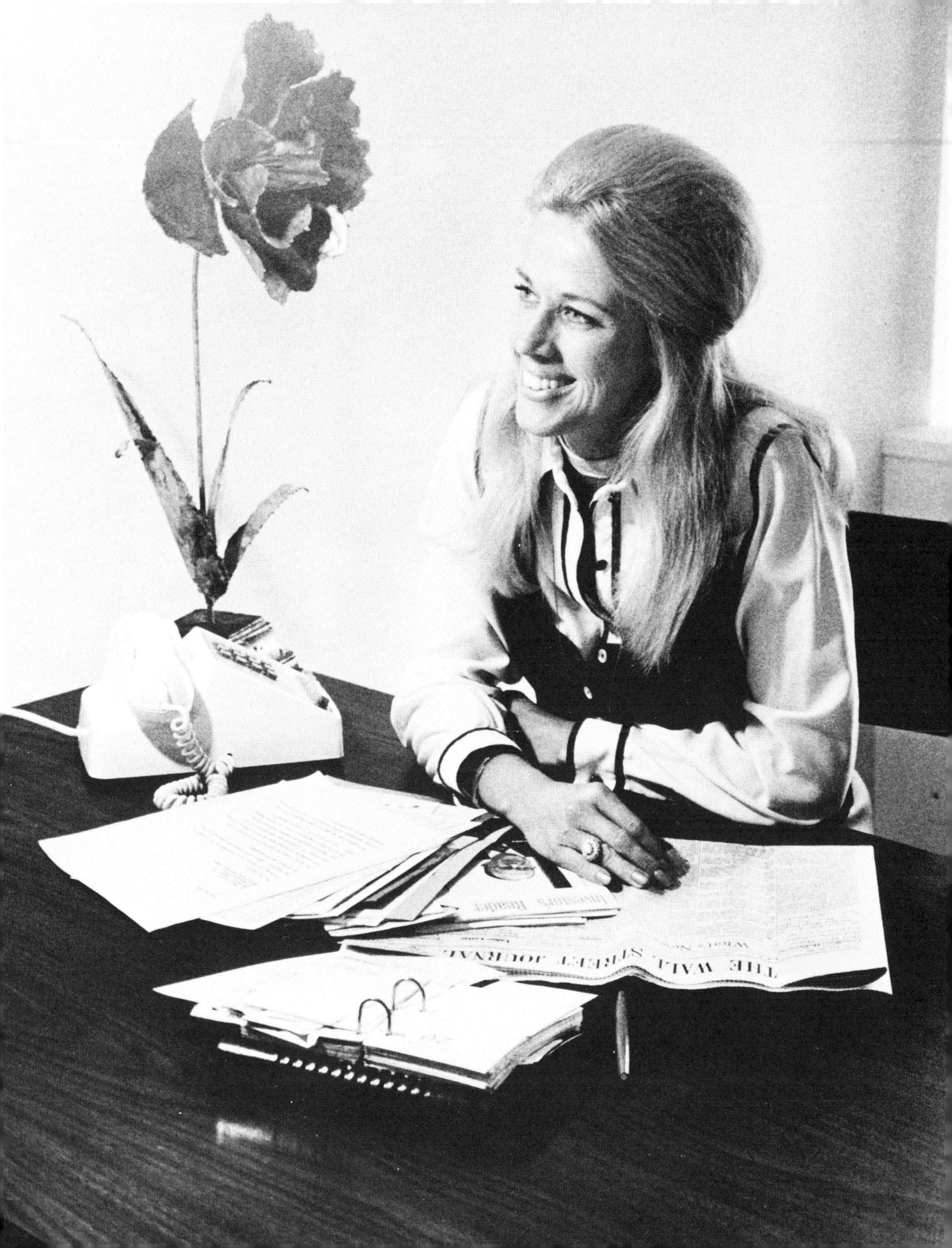

Investor's Reader
THE WALL STREET JOURNAL

Sometimes meetings with clients must be held at the client's company, which may mean either a short drive to the suburbs of my city or a short trip to New York, Texas or Canada. I guess the travel is my favorite part of the job. When I travel as a tourist I see only the sights, but when I travel on business I see how people really work and live all over the country.

I've found that I must take a different approach to business dealings with people from various parts of the country. In some areas, the style is to take things slowly, and to rush is considered rude. In others, being rushed is seen as a sign of efficiency. There are cities where one dresses casually for work and others where the most conservative dress is the rule.

As an executive, I find that my biggest responsibility is to keep things running smoothly. This means getting along with people and helping those I work with to get along with one another. In a happy office more work is done, and done better.

In dealing with clients, we meet mainly with their presidents and top executives. Sometimes men I am meeting with for the first time express surprise when the marketing vice-president they are expecting is a woman. They are more used to dealing with men. But as we work together and they see that I know my job, they quickly get used to the idea.

I feel that marketing is a growing field. There are positions in firms like mine, and also within companies that have their own marketing departments, or in connection with advertising agencies.

Being in the business world has certainly proved to me that it's not a dull world. I've also found that one can meet and help people in more than one or two fields. In fact, as I observe people around the country, I find that in nearly every field, contact with people and the ability to get along with them is a major part of the job.

Anna K. Whitchurch   INDUSTRIAL PSYCHOLOGIST

When I started college I planned to get a degree in mathematics, which I had always liked very much. One of the requirements for the degree was a course in psychology. The professor who taught that course really made the subject live, for he loved psychology and so made it fascinating for everyone who took his course. I considered changing my major to psychology, and found that if I did, I could still make use of my interest in mathematics, for in certain areas of psychology much mathematics is used. An added bonus was that I would be more involved with people than I would have been in the study of mathematics alone.

While studying for my master's degree I married, and my husband and I attended Cornell University where we received our doctors' degrees together. One day I decided I should like to put my Ph.D. degree in psychology to work directly, and I began looking for a job in the field of industrial psychology. I was fifty years old at the time, and most of my experience had been in teaching. Although I had kept up in my field by reading, I wondered what my chances were, and whether I would face discrimination because of my age and the fact that I am a woman.

This difficulty did not happen for the president of the firm I applied to had great respect for women; his mother was a surgeon. It also happened that he valued maturity and was looking for just that in applicants for the position.

I have been with my firm now for twenty-five years and enjoy my work tremendously. What an industrial psychologist does, basically, is to help companies match the right person and job. We study the needs of a company, find out what kind of personnel it needs, test people for jobs and test employees to see if they are suited to the jobs they hold or would be happier in a different area of the company. We help people see their strengths and weaknesses, which is the first step for them to make in using their strengths and overcoming their weaknesses.

The most challenging part of this work is reviewing the results of a test with the person who has taken it. One case I particularly remember. A young man came in to my office for a review of tests he had taken, put his feet up on a chair and said, "I don't believe in these tests—they're a waste of time." I told him, "These tests will tell me why you are acting the way you are about them." I told him that, and much more about himself. He was amazed. "How can you do that?" he asked. I replied that his responses to the tests gave me a clear picture of the man who was doing the responding. Later he told someone in our office, "She certainly took me apart, but it helped me a lot."

On some occasions, insight can help as much as tests. Just observing a person gives one clues. Another young man I counseled had taken tests that showed he had aptitude for sales work and could learn quickly. He wanted a job in sales but was not being considered for it. When I entered the room I noticed he did not rise or shake hands, although he seemed to be a friendly person. I soon discovered that he had grown up in an isolated area and had had very little social contact. He simply did not know how to act with people—a major drawback in sales work. Once he learned a few social graces, he did very well.

During the last two years I have been semi-retired, coming in two days a week to help train young people who are new on our staff. I enjoy seeing them grow in their work. Working with people does seem to be what I enjoy most about my field. To think I might have missed it if that professor had not made psychology so interesting to me.

Besides my field of industrial psychology, there are several others that might interest a girl who likes psychology. A school psychologist develops special educational programs to help teachers understand children with behavior problems. School psychologists also give special tests and help teachers to spot and help children with unusual learning problems. An engineering psychologist advises designers of machines. A consumer psychologist studies why people buy what they do. One psychologist you may have come in contact with is the counselor in your school. Many school guidance counselors are psychologists. They can give you advice on careers in psychology and lists of schools that have strong programs in the field. In fact, a guidance counselor is a good person to visit no matter what your choice of career.

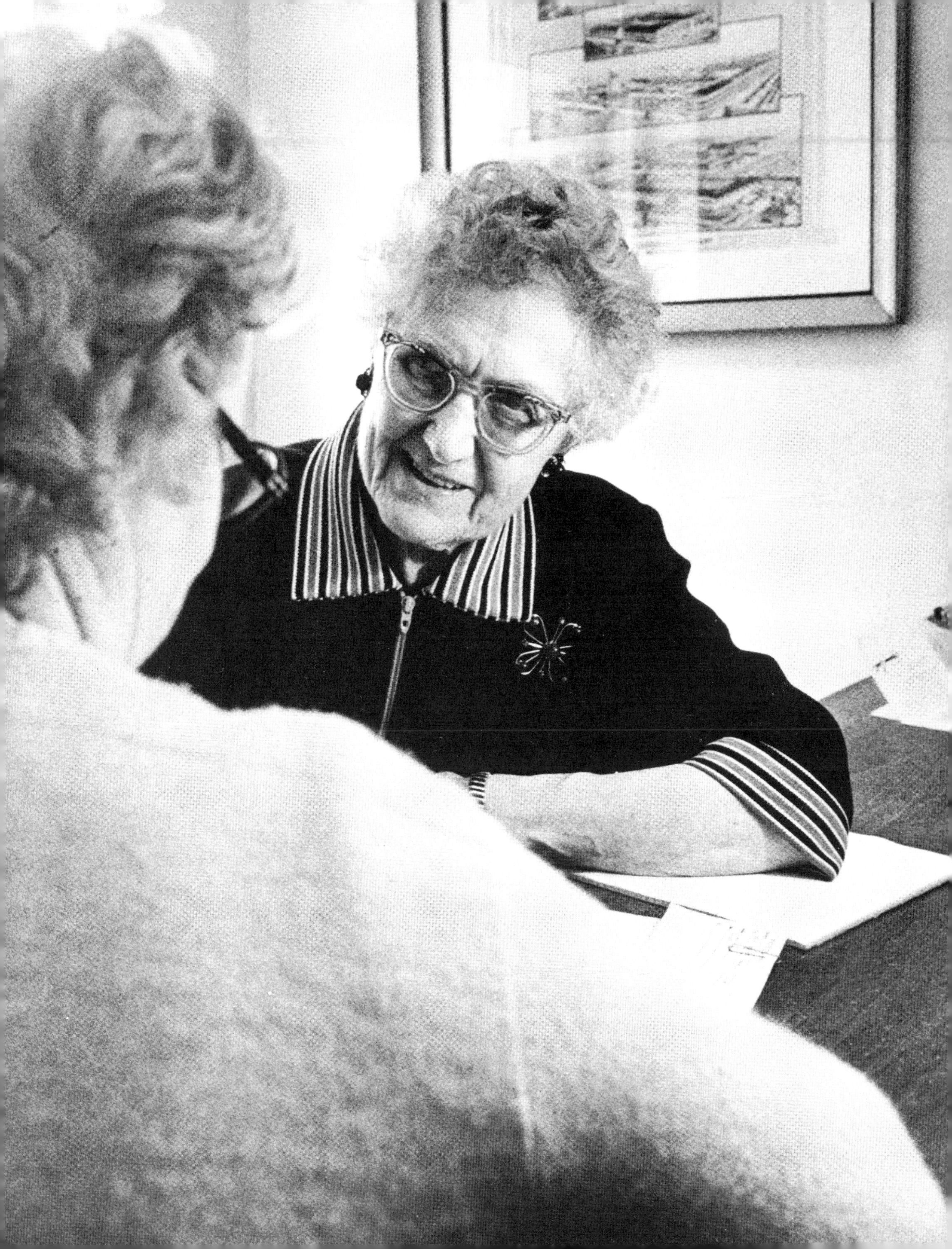

Ruth Nelson SYSTEMS ANALYST

One of the fastest-growing fields today is the field of electronic data processing—the use of computers. Computers are used in business, government, science, medicine and many other fields. They are becoming so important that college students studying business are often required to take a course in computer programming, for nearly every business uses them in some way. Even if computers become as common as typewriters, however, they will remain an interesting and challenging tool.

As important as they are, many people find computers mysterious and have no idea of what a person who works with them does. Most areas of electronic data processing are not that mysteriously technical. It is not necessary to be a mathematical wizard to work with computers; you just need a logical mind. There are people working in this field who are language majors and literature majors as well as math majors. Some have had only a little college and some have master's degrees. What is essential in the field is simply a clear, logical mind.

The field is still so new that few people agree on whether to call it a business, profession or science. In my view, each area of computer work may be classified differently. For computer programmers, the work is much like a trade while systems analysts are more like businessmen and businesswomen. One can work up from programmer to systems analyst to executive, as I have, so the whole field might be called a profession. The field is so new that none of these jobs has been completely defined yet, and the duties of each change as the field changes.

A computer is a huge calculator. It has the ability to add, subtract, multiply and divide with lightning speed. It can't "think," but with a programmer to direct it, it can use this enormous speed to process great amounts of data and help solve difficult problems. Handling information in this way is called data processing. It saves a tremendous amount of time and space. For example, in the payroll department of a large company, checks may be prepared each week to pay each of the employees. The number of hours a person worked must be multiplied by how much that person makes an hour. Then a check must be prepared showing that total and the

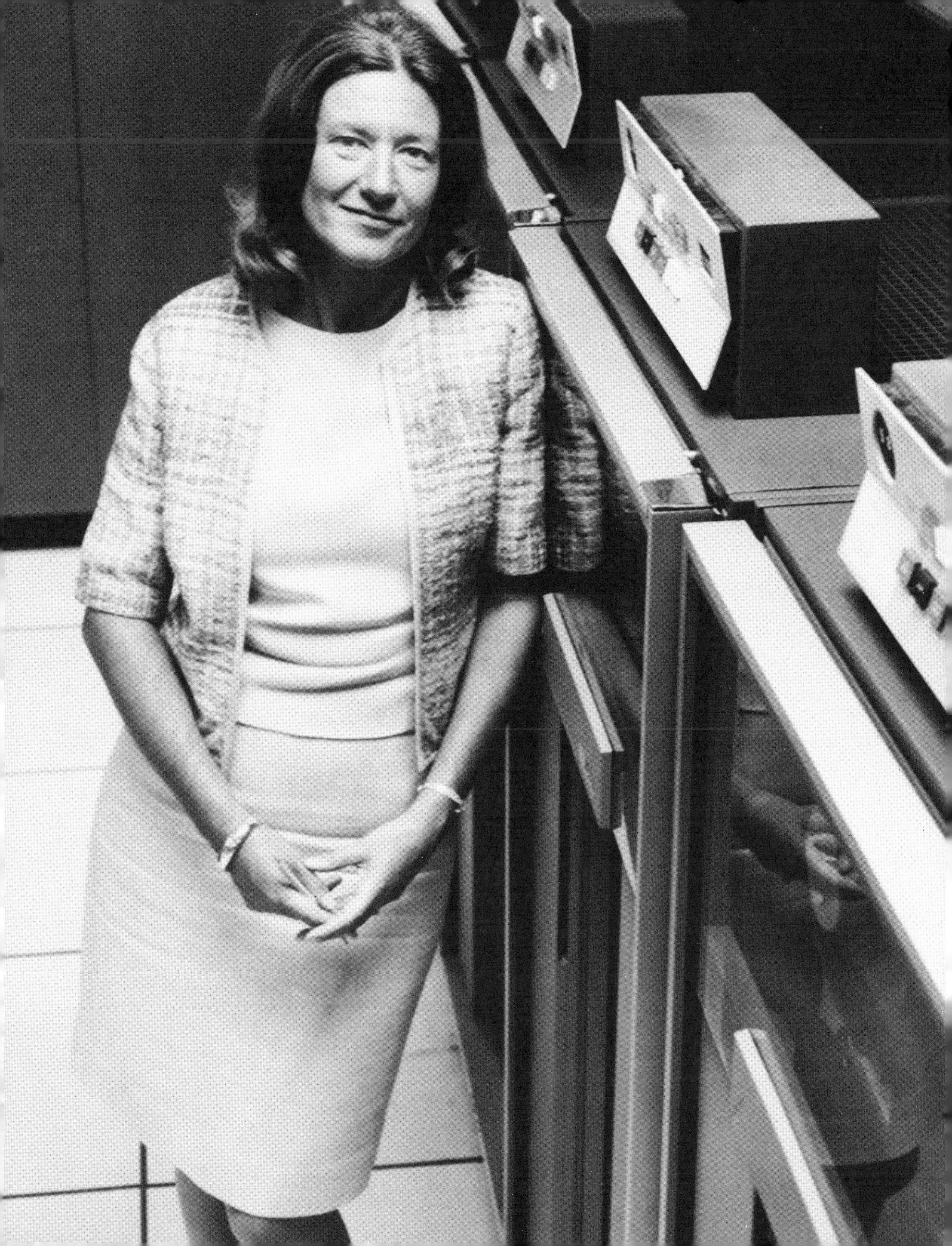

person's name. The computer can find a person's name, do this multiplication, print the total on the check, and turn out thousands of checks in a very short time.

Some of the computers at my company are programmed to prepare labels for magazines. If the records of the millions of people subscribing to these magazines were on ordinary cards, they would crowd everyone out of the building. When these records are put on computer tapes, they can fit into a small space. Computers are used in this way to streamline business.

There are many different types of computers, using different computer languages. Computer languages are made of signs and numbers; they are nothing like a spoken language. Some have interesting names such as COBOL, which stands for Common Business Oriented Language, or FORTRAN, Formula Translation, which is used for scientific computer programming.

A computer cannot do all the work it does without guidance. Careful thought is necessary in planning how to use a computer, and preparing information to be used. You must also understand something about the field you are using it for. Each phase of the process has a job that corresponds to it.

Scientists design the machines, systems analysts decide how they will be used, programmers translate the plans of the systems analysts into computer language, and more advanced programmers do complicated high-level programming.

A programmer deals mainly with computers. The job of systems analyst, however, has to do with more areas than computers. There are many different systems within an organization. For example, a business may use typewriters for correspondence, calculating machines for simple math, keypunch machines, printing machines, and many more. A systems analyst decides which part of the work can be done best by which systems, and which parts should be done without machines. There were systems analysts even before there were computers. They used to be called efficiency experts.

I enjoy working in the field of data processing for many reasons; one is that the work is done by individuals. I've heard many programmers express the feeling of satisfaction they get from doing a job entirely by themselves rather than with a committee. They identify with the systems they use in working with their particular type of computer.

Another thing I like about programming is that you always know when you've made a mistake, because when you do, the system won't come out right. Then you're able to keep on trying until you finally get it perfect. There are no maybes, only wrong or right. There may be many different ways of approaching a problem, but only one that will come out exactly right. I get great satisfaction from having done something correctly.

As a systems analyst, I enjoy designing something that will not only work, but will work in the most efficient manner. It's only through experience that I learn if something will work well or not.

Travel is a bonus I didn't expect in this line of work, and yet I've traveled quite a bit. Recently, I've made several trips to New York to oversee the transplanting of our equipment from one of our offices there to one in Chicago. Systems analysts who work for consulting firms travel much more. They may be sent to advise businesses and organizations all over the country, and sometimes to other countries. Some analysts even work free-lance—as consultants on a job-to-job basis.

Organizations that hire programmers and analysts have varying requirements. Some expect you to have a college degree, some expect only a little college. Some look for people who have studied computer science in college, some prefer to train their own personnel. Some expect you to be strong in math, but most just look for a logical mind. Those organizations that train their own personnel usually send them to a school run by the manufacturers of the kind of computer they use, or purchase a course that they give to trainees themselves. I came into my company with a college degree in business administration, and when my company first began using computers, I became more and more involved and learned as I went along.

I'm very enthusiastic about advising girls to go into this field, for it is growing fast and becoming more and more varied.

Computers are used in business, science, medicine, education and are even used in the arts. For example, some of the visual effects you may have seen on television are produced by computer, and I've heard of an experimental symphony composed by means of computer. Because of this variety, a woman can combine electronic data processing with other fields that interest her. Best of all, I feel, she can have the satisfaction of really using her mind.

Adeline Story BANK VICE-PRESIDENT

I was working as secretary to the president of a bank, doing what I felt was a good job, when suddenly one day my boss said, in a very challenging manner, "Do you just want to be a secretary here or are you interested in banking as a career?" I knew he was a man who felt that everyone should use his or her talents to the fullest and I realized I could be doing more with mine. So I took a deep breath and answered, "I'd like to try banking as a career." "Good," he said, "you're fired as my secretary and hired into our training program."

In the next year I spent a few months in each of the main areas of the bank, working as a teller in paying and receiving, in loans, in bonds and as a statement clerk. In addition, I went to the American Institute of Banking. Eventually I was promoted from assistant cashier to assistant vice-president, then to vice-president. More recently I added the duties of assistant trust officer to the vice-presidency.

To enjoy banking one must like detail work and math, and of course I do. However, the greatest satisfaction of my job comes from assisting people with financial problems and helping people who don't understand banking to become knowledgable. I recall one widowed woman who had never even learned to handle a checkbook. Gradually I taught her the details of trusts, stocks, bonds, savings and checking accounts and all the many things one must know to handle large amounts of money wisely. She learned amazingly fast and I was proud to see her gaining confidence in herself as she learned to handle her own affairs.

It seems that assisting people in this way is what attracted me to banking in the first place. I had always been impressed by the large sums of money the bank officers were responsible for. But even more, it seemed that they were really helping people—for people came into the bank worried or confused about their financial affairs, and they went out with their problems clarified or solved.

The terms used in talking about banking sometimes confuse people. For example, interest is payment for use of money borrowed. A statement is the form sent monthly from your bank to you to tell you how many checks you have written, how much money you have deposited and how much you have in the account. A trust is money held in one person's name for the benefit of another person. An officer is a person of authority in the bank. This last term has brought about some amusing confusion. When I was first made an officer of the bank, I hurried home that evening and announced to my husband and daughter, "I'm an officer!" My daughter asked, "Do you get to carry a gun?" On another occasion I had told a man to "take this form to the officer on the island for approval." I had meant the bank officer in the separate center island area of the bank. The man took it to the police officer on the traffic island in the middle of the street in front of the bank!

In my work as a trust officer of the bank I assist people by investment counseling. I help them decide how to put their money to work by investments: they loan money to a company they feel will do well and the company pays them interest for the use of their money. I keep in touch with the money markets to find out where the best rates for large sums of money are.

One of the most interesting aspects of banking is the fact that many banks have branches in several countries. In international banking you might find yourself working in several different countries while working for the same bank.

Many customers of our bank have sent their children to visit me in order to learn how banks work. I enjoy showing them around and explaining the various functions of a bank. Going along with a parent to the bank is one way to learn more about the field if it interests you, and so is working as a teller when you're older. To enter the training program of a bank it helps to have a college degree in business adminstration. Then there's also the American Institute of Banking, with branches in many major U.S. cities. In many cases, the bank you are working for pays your tuition. They teach fundamentals of banking, negotiable instruments, commercial law and accounting.

ADELINE W. STORY VICE PRESIDENT AND ASSISTANT TRUST OFFICER

FOR FURTHER INFORMATION

ACCOUNTANT
Accounting Careers Council
National Distribution Center
PO Box 650 Radio City Station
New York, New York 10019

American Institute of Certified Public Accountants
666 Fifth Ave.
New York, New York 10019

ARCHITECT
American Institute of Architects
1735 New York Ave. NW
Washington, D.C. 20006

ARTIST, ILLUSTRATOR
National Art Education Association
National Education Association
1201 16th St. NW
Washington, D.C. 20036

BANKER
American Institute of Banking
American Banking Association
1120 Connecticut Ave. NW
Washington, D.C. 20036

BIOLOGIST
American Institute of Biological Sciences
3900 Wisconsin Ave. NW
Washington, D.C. 20016

BROKER
Stock Broker
New York Stock Exchange
11 Wall St.
New York, New York 10005

(Commodities Broker)
Chicago Board of Trade
141 W. Jackson St.
Chicago, Illinois 60606

COMPUTER PROGRAMMER, SYSTEMS ANALYST
Data Processing Management Association
505 Busse Highway
Park Ridge, Illinois 60068

Association for Computing Machinery
1133 Avenue of the Americas
New York, New York 10036

ENGINEER, CITY PLANNER

American Society of Civil Engineers
345 E. 47th St.
New York, New York 10017

American Institute of Planners
917 15th St. NW
Washington, D.C. 20005

FILM MAKER

American Film Institute
The John F. Kennedy Center for the
Performing Arts
Washington, D.C. 20566

FLORIST

Small Business Administration
Washington, D.C. 20416

GEOLOGIST

American Geological Institute
2201 M St. NW
Washington, D.C. 20037

American Geophysical Union
2100 Pennsylvania Ave. NW
Washington, D.C. 20037

LAWYER

American Bar Association
1155 E. 60th St.
Chicago, Illinois 60637

MARKETING

American Marketing Association
230 N. Michigan Ave.
Chicago, Illinois 60601

American Management Association
135 W. 50th St.
New York, New York 10020

MUSICIAN

National Association of Schools of Music
1424 16th St. NW
Washington, D.C. 20036

OCEANOGRAPHER

American Society for Oceanography
854 Main Building
Houston, Texas 77002

American Society for Limnology and Oceanography
W. K. Kellogg Biological Station
Michigan State University
Hickory Corners, Michigan 49060

PHARMACIST

American Pharmaceutical Association
2215 Constitution Ave. NW
Washington, D.C. 20037

American Council on Pharmaceutical Education
77 W. Washington St.
Chicago, Illinois 60602

PHYSICIAN

Council on Medical Education
American Medical Association
535 N. Dearborn St.
Chicago, Illinois 60610

PHYSICIAN'S ASSOCIATE

American Academy of Physicians' Associates
Room 356
2150 Pennsylvania Avenue
Washington, D.C. 20037

PHYSICIST

American Institute of Physics
335 E. 45th St.
New York, New York 10017

PILOT

Air Line Pilots Association International
1329 E St. NW
Washington, D.C. 20004

PSYCHOLOGIST

American Psychological Association
1200 17th St. NW
Washington, D.C. 20036

Suzanne Seed AUTHOR, PHOTOGRAPHER

A free-lance photographer may work for a different company each day, rather than working for one. So as a free-lance photographer I can have a different boss each day, and still be my own boss. Between jobs, I work on assignments that I give myself, such as this book.

Working this way, however, I must be ready for anything. I sometimes find myself in strange places while doing my work. I may travel in a helicopter to photograph pollution, or don sterile green hospital clothes to photograph surgery. I may find myself in a warehouse freezer at forty degrees below zero doing pictures of frozen pork bellies or I may be out in the rain on the expressway taking pictures of traffic jams. I once found myself in a rowboat, photographing a huge machine that gobbles up overgrown water-lilies, trying to keep the machine from gobbling me up with the water-lilies. I've also taken pictures from the bottom of a nuclear missile silo, from cranes above buildings, from moving scaffolds in factories, and from absolute ground level—eyeball to eyeball with a grasshopper. Other days I may spend doing close-up pictures of dainty antique dolls or of the insides of a flower.

There's variety in the people I work with too. Although I sometimes photograph famous people, I'm too busy behind the camera to visit or get to know them. Occasionally I'll find that the person I'm photographing and I don't speak the same language, and I have to give directions in sign language. The subject of a picture may or may not be fun to photograph. At times, knowing how to get along with people and animals is as important as knowing how to make a good picture.

As a free lancer in any field, you are your own company. There is often insecurity in such a position, for there is no way to know how much money you will make in any particular week. In addition, you must buy your own equipment and arrange your own business matters, or hire an agent to arrange them for you. For those photographers who want steady work, there are a few jobs with magazines, many with newspapers, and some with companies that hire their own photographers. In the past, newspapers have been slow to hire women photographers, but they are beginning.

Most good photographic training emphasizes the fact that photography is both a means of communication and an art. Seeing is the first step. If you keep your eyes open to the world around you, you can't help but notice things you'd like to show to others. Showing what you see to others is where the communication comes in. To say what you want about your subject, you emphasize what drew *you* to it. Here's where you need the mechanics of photography, the way a painter needs a brush. For example: to emphasize a color, you may need a certain filter. To emphasize movement, you may need a particular film. And to emphasize details, you may need a special lens. Once you know all the technical rules of photography, you're free to break them when it helps you say what you want to say.

Some photographers prefer formal training in either photography or art in a professional school or college. Others learn by going to work for a studio photographer, helping with work in the darkroom, carrying equipment, finding props, and so forth, until they know enough to look for work on their own. Some even teach themselves. I'm partial to fine arts training as a background, probably because I went that way myself.

I was studying painting and printmaking in college, and was forced to take a course in photography. It was one of the requirements for a degree, and I didn't think I'd like it at all. But after one semester I wondered where **photography** had been all my life, for I was enjoying it more than painting. When I went looking for work after graduation, I took a portfolio of illustration and photography, and was hired as a photographer. So the choice was made for me.

I've found that photography can be as much an art as painting and printmaking were for me. And it has one special advantage to me. When I was doing more painting I can remember liking best to paint from life. No matter how abstract my work, I liked to have a real landscape, real model, or real interior in front of me. Now, as a photographer, everything I work with is there in front of me, and certainly very real.

One of my favorite jobs so far has been this book you are reading. Perhaps this is because it is the latest job, but I think that it's rather because the book is a labor of love. I know how exciting and fulfilling it is to do work you really care about, and would like my daughter and other girls to grow up discovering their own abilities and finding work they love. This is not easy for all girls, and my own daughter made me realize this. She brought home books from school that were illustrated with pictures of little girls doing nothing more interesting than sweeping floors, while the pictures showed little boys doing everything that was fun or exciting. I realized that on television she saw women portrayed in only a few jobs: nurse, secretary and teacher. I'd like girls **to know** that they, like the women in this book, can do work they love if they keep their eyes open to discovering what their own true talents are.

INDEX

Accountant 125
Actress 45
Architect 12
Axeman, Lois 48

Banker 151
Beis, Marilyn 94
Biologist, Developmental 79
Biophysicist 83
Broker, Commodities 121

Cab Driver 104
Carlson, Lynne 52
Carpenter 94
City Planner 128
Composer 16
Conductor 16
Congresswoman 116

Dailey, Irene 45
Dickey, Francine 125
Dress Designer 24

Engineer, Civil 128

Falkenberg, Charlene 91
Film Maker 41
Florist 101

Geologist 57
Ginter, Joyce 108
Goold, Mary Ann 111

Harris, Margaret 16
Harris, Sharon 24
Heise, Jan 140
Holm, Jeanne 131

Illustrator 48

Joye, Judy 65

Kerbis, Gertrude Lempp 12
Khalafalla, Aida 83
King, Margaret 104

Lafontant, Jewel 135
Laney, Mary 36

Lanyon, Ellen 27
Lawyer 135
Letter Carrier 88

McKee, Edith 57
McLain, Elizabeth 128
McLennon, Linda 88
Marketer 140
Military Service (Brigadier General) 131
Mink, Patsy Takemoto 116
Morris, Jeanne 21

Nelson, Ruth 146

Oceanographer 65
Olsen, Sandra 62
O'Neill, Maggie 98
Ovitz, Carol 121

Painter 27
Pharmacist 70
Physician 62
Physician's Associate 74
Pianist 16
Pilot 91
Policewoman 98
Psychologist, Industrial 143
Pykacek, June 31

Realtor 108
Reporter, Radio-TV 36
Rivet, Jackie 41

Sedlak, Bonnie 79
Sportswriter 21
Story, Adeline 151
Systems Analyst 146

Telephone Repairwoman 111
Theater Director 31
Tremulis, Jean 101

Vanderbilt, Clara 74
Veterinarian 52

Wahlman, Mary 70
Whitchurch, Anna K. 143

This book is set in Linotype Optima.

CARNEGIE PUBLIC LIBRARY
ROBINSON, ILLINOIS